Mary's Diary

Mary's Diary

Mary's Diary was written by David Painting, a Bible teacher and pastor with a passion to see ordinary people doing extraordinary things with God. To that end he is committed to demystifying the Bible, making it accessible and reconnecting people with its message. David writes: "My hope in presenting this 'diary' is that readers will become excited again in the reality of God's love and His tenacity in using ordinary people to demonstrate and be recipients of that love. I hope too that it will inspire many to re-read the gospels and indeed to read scripture with fresh eyes. Above all of course, I want everyone to know Jesus personally, to begin the eternal adventure that is relationship with God."

David is currently Executive Pastor at Stopsley Baptist Church in Luton, UK.

David Painting

Mary's Diary

Published by David Painting

Additional copies from www.lulu.com

Mary's Diary

Copyright © 2008 David Painting

All rights reserved.

ISBN 978-1-4466-7228-0

Contents

About Mary's Diary

Part 1: Annunciation   -   extracts 1 - 10

Part 2: Incarnation   -   extracts 11 - 24

Part 3: Refugees   -   extracts 25 - 34

Part 4: Childhood   -   extracts 35 - 41

Part 5: Messiah   -   extracts 42 - 86

Part 6: Kingdom   -   extracts 87 - 100

About Mary's Diary

Mary's Diary is a work of imagination. It is highly unlikely that Mary would have been able to write and even if she had, no record of an actual diary exists! That said, this is not in essence a work of fiction. It is rooted in the Gospels written by Luke and to a lesser extent, John. It is researched with regards the cultural context of the time and my imagination has been restricted to a thorough Biblical framework.

Each chapter consists of a number of diary extracts which form a significant development of the story. At the end of each chapter there is a Bible reference which points to the scriptural background to that part of the 'diary' along with some thoughts that take you 'behind the diary'. You may find it helpful to read the diary extracts in the morning, (it will rarely take more than five minutes) then allow the material to percolate during the day before reading the relevant passage and considering the 'behind the diary' thoughts.

If you have friends who are reading it or a small group, you might want to share what God has spoken to you or pray together. Alternatively there is a forum on the web site (www.marysdiary.net) on which you can comment and engage with others who are reading.

Part 1 - Annunciation

Birthday

Extract 1
I was 14 yesterday! All my friends were there - and my family of course. It was wonderful, I don't normally like being the centre of attention, but yesterday was special. That's why I'm starting this diary! For so long it's been 'You shouldn't be learning to write - that's only for priests and Levites' Then finally, yesterday - my own pen - given to me by my most fervent critic - my Father! And some parchment from the man who taught me - Uncle Zechariah. Well, he is a priest so who could argue! So here I am, 14 years old, writing my own diary - what a year it will be, my last as a single woman - but who will be the lucky man? Dear diary, you will be the first to know - who will marry Mary?

Extract 2
Well, it seems the choice has come down from four to two. Ruben has been promised to Leah! Imagine that - all along we thought she was to marry Simeon, then last night Samuel & Isaac were seen falling out of the inn together and this morning Isaac announces the 'good' news. Leah's mum was furious! Well, she is quite a big lady and Simeon will be the baker! I don't know how Leah feels but I'm just happy that Ruben is out of the picture - I've never really wanted to be a farmer's wife!

Extract 3
Father's mad at Samuel - he says that everyone's plans and years of negotiating have been thrown into confusion. Mum says that he's just worried he will have to spend more than he had planned on my dowry. Sometimes I wish I could just be married and have my own place right now, all the arguing and haggling over status and money. It's not like we're ever going to be noticed anyway - who's going to care in Nazareth!

Part 1 - Annunciation

Even more depressing is that we can't now afford to go up to Jerusalem for Passover - everyone else is going - all my friends. Our last chance to go together as a family and we get to stay home. I'm beginning to get mad at Samuel & Isaac myself now.

Extract 4
We went anyway! It was just as I remembered, the gold, the temple, the people! But as always, just the amazing sense of holiness, of God close by. When we sung the final Psalm it was as if God himself was with us - I closed my eyes and I could see the Egyptians chasing after us, I could hear the hooves, the battle cries. I could feel the fear as we crushed forward, sure that we would drown. Then the cries of Hosanna as the sea parted and we crossed in safety to this wonderful land. Uncle Zech thought I'd had too much of the wine, but I hadn't (well, maybe just a little!).

Extract 5
In the end it wasn't my health that they should have worried about. Old Abel the carpenter died last night on the way back. He'd had a fever all the time we were there, but he seemed to be getting better. The first we knew was when we heard the wailing of the mourners. I liked Abel - he scared me when I was younger - he looked frightening with his broken teeth and the scar he got when the old tower collapsed. But he was kind in the strong way that builders have. Not an angry strength, but a gentle strength. He reminded me of God. I'll miss Abel.

Extract 6
Father seems annoyed with Abel! He seems annoyed a lot of the time right now. He says that it will only mean more change. Of course we will need a new carpenter so we are to have Jacob's son from Bethlehem. Joseph (the son) has just finished his apprenticeship - why he's agreed to come here no-one is saying. Apparently he isn't married though which given his age must mean something.

Part 1 - Annunciation

Extract 7

I know why he's agreed to come. It's my father. Or some friend of a relative who knows my father. I can't believe it. Not Ruben or Simeon or James. I'm going to marry a carpenter from Bethlehem called Joseph. He must be at least 50. And ugly. And a bad carpenter. Suddenly farmers seem attractive. He arrives next week.

Part 1 - Annunciation

Behind the Diary

Because Mary is given such prominence in some parts of the Church, others tend to downplay her role. But here she is, a young girl, no doubt more mature out of necessity than someone this age might be in today's western society, but all the same, a young girl. She doesn't yet know the pivotal role she will play in human history. She just wants to know something of her future.

Do you remember those days of simplistic faith? Those days of youth when everything seemed possible? Remember how quick we were to judge others by the outward? When we were inevitably right?

Spend some quiet moments before God on your own - ask Him to blow away the cobwebs of 'maturity' that are really a mask for unbelief! Let's encourage one another back to a place of child-like simplicity, not childishness.

Of course, we don't know how Joseph ended up in Nazareth or the details of the marriage arrangements between him and Mary. But from what we do know of the story, explore in your group the version in the 'diary'. How does it explain the facts, how does thinking this through connect us with the reality of the story?

Part 1 - Annunciation

Joseph

Extract 8

I saw him today. I didn't want to go but the whole town went out to greet the new carpenter. They haven't stopped talking about him since the news first broke. 'Joseph' this and 'Joseph' that. You'd think the Emperor was coming to Nazareth. 'You're so lucky' all the mothers keep telling me. That's not what my friends think. I know I should be grateful to father - I know it's a good match - I marry a respectable business man - I'll never be poor - and father hasn't had to pay too much for the dowry. I know I didn't really like any of the boys here, but at least I knew them.

Anyway, I saw him. And the strangest thing happened. I was deliberately at the back of the crowd, sort of looking the other way. And he looked at me and I found I couldn't look away. He's big and strong and I think he's kind - like Abel - and we looked at one another for what seemed like an age. Then he got off his donkey and pushed through the crowd - ignoring all the important men - and stood in front of me and laughed! I felt embarrassed for a moment, then I realised he wasn't laughing at me, but with me - then I was laughing too. Finally he spoke: 'So, Mary, now I know why I am in Nazareth'. Then he turned and was gone. I love him! I'm going to marry Joseph the carpenter!

Extract 9

He is kind, and strong and not ugly at all! He's a good carpenter too, he made me a lovely box to keep my diary and writing things in! And he isn't 50 - he's only a few years older than me - I still don't know why he isn't married - but he soon will be! To me! I'm so excited - I'm every bit as silly about it as my friends have been at their wedding. I used to think they were so immature! Now the whole family (even my brothers) are busy planning and preparing. Six months, that's all - who knows, if God blesses us, I could have a family of my own by the end of next year.

Part 1 - Annunciation

Behind the Diary

We often think of gender roles as a modern issue, especially in our western culture. We wonder how men can be men whilst allowing women to take a leading role when appropriate? But it isn't a new issue! Here is Mary, with a pivotal role to play in human history and Joseph called to play a significant, but supporting role. At this stage of the story neither knows it yet, they are still filled with preconceived notions of what the future might bring, the possibilities limited to their existing worldview.

We know now that God is able to do 'far more abundantly than we even think or imagine'. How do you see your future? Constrained by circumstances? Limited by cultural expectations? The truth is that when we allow God to be involved in our life glass ceilings are shattered, human barriers are broken, the impossible is within reach.

What is it that God is asking of you? What is his call on your life? Don't be afraid, reach out and touch the stars.

Part 2 - Incarnation

Gabriel

Extract 10

Oh God. I've just read the last entry. It seems a lifetime ago. Was it really yesterday I was writing about having children? Now everything has changed. Yesterday I was a girl wanting to be a woman. Now I'm - I don't know.

Last night, before I went to bed, I was in my room. I was just stood there, thinking about the future, enjoying the happiness of it all. Then he came. Not Joseph, he wouldn't do such an improper thing. Not anyone I knew. Not anyone. An angel - a messenger from God - Gabriel himself. He stood there, in our house, in Nazareth. I thought I'd gone mad, fallen asleep, dreaming. But somehow it was more real than real and suddenly I was frightened. Not like with Abel, just his sheer presence, his realness - I don't know.

Then he spoke, he told me not to be afraid. He said that I had found favour with God. He said God wanted me to have his son. I blurted the first thing that came into my head - 'I'm not even married yet, I'm a virgin - how can that be?'. I realised immediately how foolish it was, but Gabriel smiled and told me what I knew, that with God all things are possible. He said that God's Spirit would come upon me and that I would become pregnant. Then he stopped and waited. I realised he was waiting for an answer. He wasn't telling me what had happened, he was asking permission so that it could happen. I remembered Passover, I remembered God's presence, I remembered the promises he had made to bring salvation to the world. I was overwhelmed by the privilege, the sense of worth. I said yes.' Yes, let it be to me as you have said'. He nodded and told me incredible news. Elizabeth, Uncle Zech's wife (who must be at least 50 - no really) was 6 months pregnant with their first child!

Part 2 - Incarnation

While I was working that out, he left. Disappeared. Just me in the room with all the family noise going on outside and even more noise inside my head.

Extract 11
I have to see Elizabeth. If she's pregnant, I'll know it wasn't a dream. I can't even begin to start thinking about what this means till I know for sure. It seemed so real, but even now when I read the words it seems distant, so unlikely, so unbelievable. Yet when I close my eyes, I can see him, hear him, sense God's presence through him.

I told the family that I have to visit Elizabeth - I didn't explain why, I can hardly believe it myself. I've never 'told' them anything before in my life. But I'm a woman now - more than that, a woman contracted to be married, no longer under their authority. I had to get permission from Joseph of course - how I'll miss him! But even more painful is the fact that I can't say anything to him yet. I have to know first; yet I need him, his strength, his kindness, his reassurance, his love. So I'm packed, some friends are coming most of the way with me, so I'll be safe.

In a couple of days time I'll know.

Part 2 - Incarnation

Behind the Diary

Luke 1:26-38

The whole plan for the salvation of the world hinges on this young girl's choice. As in the story of Esther - Mordecai points out to her that if she will not risk acting, then she and all that generation of Jews would be killed. God would then find another way of saving some, but 'who knows that you might have been brought to this point, for such a time as this'. So with Mary. If she says 'no' God will find another way, another person in another generation perhaps. But the time is ripe now, salvation hope can enter the world now. And Gabriel and the universe wait for this young girl as she counts the cost and 'ponders these things in her heart'. This is why God chose her, because He knows that she understands His character. 'Love does not insist on its own way'. He needs a mother for His son who will teach this love, God's way, by word and deed.

And so He waits. As He did in Eden, God once more submits His omnipotence to the decision of frail humanity. This time a young virgin will say 'yes' to the Father of light, fulfilling the prophecy to Eve - 'from your seed will come one who will tread on his head'.

This is the extraordinary significance God places in you. You get to choose. Your choices have profound significance now and into eternity. Choices that lead to truth and light and life or choices that bring deceit, darkness and death - for you and for those you are in community with.

As God invites you to fulfill the unique call on your life, the angels, the enemy, the universe pauses, holding its breath. Will you today, now, choose life?

Part 2 - Incarnation

Notes:-

Part 2 - Incarnation

Elizabeth

Extract 12
I've never been so nervous in all my life as I was when I knocked on the door. So much resting on what I see when Elizabeth opens it. So much confusion inside me:

'Lord, please let her be pregnant, let it not have been a dream. Oh God, please don't let her be pregnant, let me go back to just being Mary, engaged to Joseph.'

There, it's done, the door knocked. A shout from inside, someone sees me from a window. 'It's Mary' someone says. A confusion of voices, then the door swings open. Elizabeth stands there, I can't get passed her - she's too big already. Then somehow I'm inside and I shout 'Elizabeth'. Suddenly she grasps herself as her baby jumps - I go to help her but she just laughs at me, then almost bows: 'Why is this granted to me that the mother of my Lord should come to me?' That's when it hit me. It's all true. I am pregnant - it isn't a game, it isn't something happening in a story. It's me - I can't begin to understand why, but it's me and I am humbled beyond words.

Extract 13
Days and weeks of talking, of remembering, of praying. Trying to understand. Elizabeth told me their story - it's so funny! Of course we all knew they'd been praying for children for years (didn't realise they were still praying!). Nothing had happened, but then we'd got used to God not speaking to us - it's 400 years since the last prophet spoke to Israel - which is why I'd always seen a heaviness, a weariness in Uncle Zech's eyes. The rituals must have become pretty empty sometimes - I know they have for most of my friends. Anyway, it was his turn to go into the Holy place in the temple for the evening sacrifice and as usual a group of people had gathered to watch (the usual suspects - the ones showing off their holiness and the visitors who haven't seen

Part 2 - Incarnation

that nothing happens!). Except that this time something did happen! Gabriel appeared to Uncle Zech! He said that their prayers had been heard and that he and Elizabeth would have a son who would prepare the way for our Messiah! Uncle Zech couldn't believe it (or maybe wouldn't allow himself to believe it - Gabriel is pretty believable - I should know!). Anyway, Uncle Zech came out and he still can't speak so the details aren't all that clear, but one thing's for sure - Elizabeth is going to have a baby!

Extract 14

I'm going home tomorrow. It's been three months. I don't need the sight of Elizabeth's bump to confirm my own condition any more. I feel sick every morning, I haven't bled for three turns and if I look carefully, I can see the difference in my body. It's all frighteningly real. I know I have all the wonderful things that Gabriel said 'He will be great and called the Son of the Most High' and the words Elizabeth prophesied: 'Blessed are you among women' and even the words that I prayed 'He who is mighty will do great things'. All this and more and they are wonderfully comforting and at times really exciting. And I know more with every passing day how privileged I am to have his son in me.

But how will I tell Joseph?

Part 2 - Incarnation

Behind the Diary

Luke 1:39-56

Father, Son and Holy Spirit. Three unique members of this family we call God. Each fully with the nature of the other, each completely at one in vision, values and character. One God, three persons, eternally in loving relationship. It was this love that motivated them to create us in the first place. It was love that prevented them from destroying us when we chose to reject that love. Now for our sake, God is willing even to allow the nature of this triune relationship to be changed. As with all metaphors, it breaks down and becomes absurd if pushed too far - how does God pray to himself, if God is everywhere, how can He be in one place etc. But what this part of the story shows is that something changed. In some way, God is willing for our sake to allow change within the Godhead. Jesus, the Son of God - fully God Himself, lays aside His rights and His position. Omnipresent God allows Himself to be constrained to this young woman's womb. The Holy Spirit centres himself within John who is in Elizabeth's womb. Father, Son and Holy Spirit, forever one, eternally bound in the love that defines them, now in some way separate. Feeling the loneliness, the isolation that we feel. And then Mary with Jesus enters the room with Elizabeth/John/Holy Spirit. The joy of this reunion! The recognition, Son of God, Holy Spirit - no wonder the baby leaps. How much God sacrifices in this redemptive plan. Spend some time reflecting on the fullness of all that God has done to set you free.

Of course the reality of being part of God's plan is different to the thought of it! Now the reality hits Mary. The cost that was a theory now has to be paid. Will others believe, will others share in the joy of being part of His plan? God believes that the joy of us being redeemed to His love makes the price worth paying. Allow this to permeate our thought processes. The price is worth it because the prize of God's love is overwhelming.

Part 2 - Incarnation

Notes:-

Part 2 - Incarnation

Telling Joseph

Extract 15

It's awful. At first it was lovely - everyone pleased to see me again, lots of hugs - the wonderful sense of being part of family. But in my heart I kept wondering if they would share my joy at what God had done. Eventually I got some time with Joseph. Everyone thought we were catching up and planning for the wedding. The wedding that isn't going to happen now. At first he thought it was some kind of girls' story. Then when he realised I was serious, when he looked at me and knew, then he was angry. 'An angel, sure he was an angel'. But it wasn't his anger that broke my heart. It was his disappointment, the thought that I'd betrayed him. 'Do you know how rare it is for men and women to actually love each other when the marriage is arranged? I thought we had that Mary. Everyone said you were special, said you loved God, loved what was right.'

I had no words - what could I say that I hadn't already said? I couldn't bear his pain. What a fool to think that others would share my joy. All they see is the shame, all they assume is the worst. And why not? Wouldn't I? Tears aren't enough to express how I feel. 12 weeks from joy to devastation. Where are your promises now God? All those words fell to the ground as I looked into his eyes and saw his heart break in two. He's a good man, maybe the best of men. Even in his despair he wanted to spare me. He'll visit my Father tomorrow and agree the terms of the divorce. He said he'll do it quietly - I'll have to leave Nazareth of course - it won't be safe to be here branded as a harlot.

All generations will call me blessed? Right now my name is a curse.

Part 2 - Incarnation

Extract 16

Joseph arrived at the house early, I didn't see his face, couldn't bear to look. I heard my mother open the door. 'Good morning Ann', his voice sounded calmer than I expected. I waited, dreading what was next, the conversation with my Father, the shouting, the shame. I'd already packed, though I had no idea where to go other than to Elizabeth - I knew she would shelter me, even with their new baby, but I didn't know if Uncle Zech being a priest could allow it. But the storm never came. 'Can I see Mary' he asked. We walked together, I fearing some onslaught, some accusation, something even worse than was already waiting. But he turned and looked me in the eye and said quietly. 'I saw him Mary - I saw Gabriel last night. He told me that I should have trusted you, that it is all true, that you are carrying God's son. He asked me to be his earthly father. To be your husband. Mary, I love you, will you marry me?' I almost fell, the relief flooded through me - whatever happened now, I had my Joseph, my kind, strong Joseph to be by my side.

Extract 17

In the next few weeks I learned just how much I needed that kind strength. Of course, going ahead with the wedding, marrying someone who was more and more clearly pregnant meant only one thing in people's minds. I had slept with someone, that was for sure. If it hadn't been Joseph, then he would have divorced me. But he was marrying me - a clear sign of guilt. Both of us were sharing the blame, taking the punishment for something we had not done. Now of course the wedding preparations were very different. No-one could be seen to sully themselves attending the wedding of such sinners. All my childhood dreams of a wonderful wedding under a canopy with my friends and family celebrating had turned to dust. Hard enough to find a priest who would even marry us in private. But there it was, done - and yet, somehow more special than I can say. Just Joseph, me and God, exchanging vows whilst His son listened and grew inside me. Today I married the carpenter from Bethlehem!

Part 2 - Incarnation

Behind the Diary

Matthew 1: 18-23

How do you hold on to the promises of God when they seem far away? Jonah called to be a prophet, imprisoned in the stomach of a great fish. Saul, called to bring light, blind and helpless. Peter called to plant churches, running from a servant girl. Joseph called to be a leader of nations, a slave in prison. Mary called to be mother to the saviour of the world rejected by those she loved.

Yet, if we hold on, if we will have faith the very thing the enemy was using to defeat us becomes a tool to better equip us for his defeat. Jonah learns the mercy of God and a nation is transformed, what Saul sees is transformed and Paul, the apostle to the gentiles is born. Peter discovers that the rock is not his strength, but God's and the church is established, Joseph learns servant leadership and a nation is rescued. Mary learns how to handle rejection and one day, through her, the Son of God would learn it too.

What promises seem far away for you right now? So often it is at the point they seem farthest away they are closest. Hold on and you too will see the salvation of God.

Part 2 - Incarnation

Notes:-

Part 2 - Incarnation

Bethlehem

Extract 18
I'd hoped that once I was married people would slowly accept me again. Especially my Father, my daddy who gave me this pen, who couldn't now bear to look upon me. But instead, as my baby grows, so does the hatred. Its affected Joseph too - there's even talk of getting Abel's son to come back. Some weeks there's barely enough work for us to eat. It's become so bad that I hardly go out - yesterday some boys picked up stones to throw at me and Joseph had to chase them away. Then, today the news arrived that anyone with an income has to register in their home town to make sure they're paying the right taxes to Rome. Given all the rest of our troubles it seems of little consequence. Most men in Nazareth will just go to Levi our tax-gatherer but Joseph will have to go to Bethlehem - his home town. Its 70 miles and the roads aren't always safe, he will be gone at least a week and I will be on my own in a town where some people want me dead.

Extract 19
We argued - the first time in 5 months of marriage. In the end I won, I'm going to go - we're going to go with him. I know it seems crazy, two weeks of traveling when I am almost due. But being pregnant with God's son is crazy anyway, and God gave me my strong, kind Joseph for a reason - and it wasn't to leave me at the mercy of these people I once knew so well. So, I'm packed, this time there are no goodbyes, just a quick look round our first home, then close the door, hoping it will still be here when we get back.

Extract 20
Tonight is the first night that I've been able to write anything. We stopped early because I have a stomach ache - all the walking I guess. Anyway, it means that it is still light enough to write a little. It's been a difficult journey - I'm still sure that it was right to come - I have peace in my heart about it. But it's been hard -

Part 2 - Incarnation

tomorrow will be our fourth day, Joseph thinks we should make Bethlehem before dark. He seems nervous - we know news of my 'condition' will have reached his family - we don't know how they will react when we arrive on their doorstep. But even if they are ashamed of us, who could turn away their son and his wife when she so needs a normal bed? I'll have to stop now my stomach-ache is too uncomfortable for writing.

Extract 21
I know this is Mary's diary, but I have to do something. My wife is in labour and no-one will help. My own family shut the door on us. The inn-keeper said he was too busy. I feel so helpless. I'm a carpenter, I know nothing about this. This is a time for family, for sisters, for mothers. So I write and put down more straw and keep the animals away and stop people staring. Have they lost their sense of God? Have they forgotten compassion? We're supposed to treat strangers, foreigners better than this! All they see is what they think is sin, blind to their own wounds, they hurt others. And every cry Mary makes breaks my heart again.

Part 2 - Incarnation

Behind the Diary

Luke 2: 1-5

Hospitality is perhaps the most foundational value in the Kingdom of God because it is at the heart of who God is. This triune God in eternal loving relationship, this omnipotent God who could so easily exclude those who rejected Him, instead opens His arms and welcomes us in. The ultimate expression of hospitality is His willingness to allow us in and those who have experienced that privilege must reflect that same openness. The Bible is threaded through with this theme. From cities of refuge to the courts of the temple. From the commands regarding foreigners to Jesus' words about visiting the sick, the prisoner, offering a cup of water 'to the least of these'. The judgment on Sodom and Gomorrah was not the result of immorality (awful though that was) but because of the people's lack of hospitality towards the angelic strangers.

No surprise then that hospitality is at the heart of the incarnation story. We don't know what family Joseph still had in Bethlehem, whether they were close or not. We don't know whether Bethlehem was overrun with visitors as in the traditional view, or whether the more likely historical view in the 'diary' was the case. It matters little. The rejection of the family in Nazareth is the opposite of how we are supposed to respond. The poignant and pointed words in Luke 'there was no room at the inn' tell the whole story. Why did they need an inn? What stranger turns away a frightened man and a vulnerable girl in labour? What guest in an inn wouldn't give up their room for such a couple?

If God makes way for us in the very heart of the trinity, surely, surely we can make space for Him when His mother and surrogate father so need a room? Who is the stranger, the dispossessed, the vulnerable, the outcast that God is pointing you towards? Will you make room for them in your busy life, your crowded schedule, your overstretched bank account, at your table, in your home, in your heart?

Part 2 - Incarnation

Notes:-

Part 2 - Incarnation

Emmanuel

Extract 22

At last, a moment to write! What a night! From pain and shame and despair to extraordinary joy. It seemed like he would never be born, couldn't be born, him too big, me too small. All that pain, seeming to go on forever, forgetting what normal was like. Just like these last months. More and more rejection, more and more pain - almost losing hope that I could ever have joy again. But here he is, joy to the world, the Lord is here. Jesus is here. God is with us. Hope and my son were born tonight.

Extract 23

I've just finished feeding him again, now Joseph has him. He looks so proud - our child, yet not our child, God's child - maybe everyone's child. The shepherds certainly thought so! We thought a mob had gathered to come and kill us - nothing would have surprised me tonight. But it wasn't it was the shepherds from the sacrifice fields - where they keep the flocks for the temple. I think they'd be drinking; they were shouting and singing, babbling on about angels and bright lights in the sky. At first I wanted them to go away - we'd been on our own through the pain of this whole thing, why couldn't we enjoy this part together. But I had this quiet sense inside me that this is how it will be - Jesus has come for everyone. And then I was glad that they were ordinary shepherds. Real people who understand hardship, loneliness, being ostracised. I liked them and anyway, who can resist a newborn baby! But if they were a little drunk, the moment passed. Something changed when they saw Jesus. Maybe they recognised him, maybe there's something about him that reminded them of the angels they had just seen. But they became quiet and one by one bowed before him in reverence. In many ways, it made me more in fear than when I thought we were about to be killed. This Jesus, my Jesus - tonight it felt like the whole universe turns on you. O Lord, help me.

Part 2 - Incarnation

Extract 24
We're not going back, not yet anyway. The shepherds took us to a place where we can stay - it's so small, and there are broken timbers and holes in the roof - I guess that's why no-one lives here. But I know someone who can fix those things, and I can make us a home! Maybe, just maybe we can begin to have a normal life.

Part 2 - Incarnation

Behind the Diary

Luke 1:6-20

Time to step back and look at the bigger picture. The enemy has always been impressed with God's attributes - His power, His majesty, His knowledge. But he has never understood God's character. He makes the mistake that we so readily make - that if God can do something, He must therefore do it. When he rebelled he feared what God could do, so when He didn't, Satan assumed that he had somehow got away with it. Satan did not understand grace, did not understand mercy and did not understand that God longs for us to turn, of our own accord, acknowledging the wrongness of our choice. Did not understand that God gives us time, contrives opportunity, provides protection from our folly, waiting and hoping for our return, longing above all else, that we might reply to His hospitality with true repentance and love. In the end of course 'God is not mocked', ultimately there will be justice for those who persist in their blind rejection of who God is. But Satan never understood this, cannot conceive that God who is infinitely more powerful than he, would set aside His rights as God and become a helpless baby. It is the same mistake Peter would make - to make God in our image - and therefore provokes the response 'get behind me Satan'. The only conclusion that Satan can arrive at is that he might be able to win. The father of lies deceives himself. But as he sees glimpses of God's plan he fights back. He uses Zechariah's unbelief to try and derail the plan. He hopes Mary will say no, but she will not. He uses Joseph's disappointment to press for Mary's execution, but Joseph chooses a quiet divorce. He uses Caesar's greed to have Mary left alone where she will be vulnerable, but they decide to go together. He uses the religious 'righteousness' of the people to stir up hatred and rejection so that the baby might die in child-birth. Yet at every point God takes that which was sown for harm and uses it, through faith to bring life! Zechariah's silence made him unfit for work and robbed him of the joy of telling the good news. But it gives more time at home to conceive a baby! Driving through the census only

Part 2 - Incarnation

results in bringing the couple to Bethlehem - the heart of messianic prophecy. Seeing God's love in the midst of rejection would ultimately equip them to parent this child to be 'a man of sorrows, rejected by men'. This is the victory! Lift up your eyes to see the battle that rages, then lift them higher to 'see from whence does my help come'. Be aware of the battle, the strategies of the enemy, then give thanks to God for the overwhelming victory that He has won through this Christ-child.

Indeed - 'hope and my son were born tonight'.

Part 3 - Refugees

Simeon

Extract 25

Jerusalem is just 4 miles away, so today we went to the temple to dedicate Jesus to God. The shepherds wanted to give us a sheep for the sacrifice, but we knew that the thank-offering had to cost us something. Right now we can't afford anything really, so we bought a pair of doves and trusted that God would understand. The temple was crowded as usual, the courts for women and foreigners taken over as ever by the traders, eventually we came to present Jesus.

As we pressed forward a man came up to us - we found out later his name was Simeon and that God had revealed to him years ago that he would see the Christ before he died. It seems that he has been looking for him every day since. I had noticed him earlier - almost blind and clearly looking for something as if he had just lost it. It was quite funny to watch! I was a little worried when he looked our way. It was as if his eyes could suddenly see, he drew a deep breath and rushed towards us. Before I knew it he had taken Jesus from me and held him up as you would an offering. Joseph was about to wrestle him to the ground when he spoke some amazing words.

'Now let your servant depart in peace, for I have seen with my own eyes the salvation of my God'.

I only waited for Jesus for 9 months. These people had been waiting for him for decades, never losing hope, never giving up. For me and for them, God's promise is baby in your arms real!

Part 3 - Refugees

Extract 26

It's so long since I wrote, but it's been so busy! The shepherds story spread and people saw how well Joseph fixed the house - gradually we've begun to build a life - small group of friends, enough work so that we can eat. Every now and again the longing for my family rises up and hurts. To see Jesus growing and them not to see him. They'd be so proud. I hear news from time to time - it just distresses me more. Of course, most of the time is taken in feeding, cleaning, making the home.

But just sometimes, I cry a little.

Part 3 - Refugees

Behind the diary

Luke 2: 35-40

So many times God highlights ordinary people doing ordinary things. Even the famous people spend most of their lives in the ordinary; Adam & Eve walking and working in the garden. Abraham as a nomad for over 100 years. Moses 80 years old before he steps into the role he was called to. And here with Simeon. An old man who at some point in his past (and we suspect early in his life) had received a promise from God. One which must have seemed increasingly unlikely as the years wore on. At a time when God had not spoken prophetically to the nation for 400 years it must have sounded odd even to Simeon that God would speak to him. Interesting to speculate on what his friends might have thought or said: 'Seen the messiah today Simeon?'. People gently mocking the crazy old eccentric who no longer has anything to offer.

Yet day by day he simply did what he had always done. The daily round, the common task - everyday life. And part of that was worship. It is in worship that we remind ourselves of the goodness and greatness of God. We expose ourselves again to the reality of His faithfulness. Paul tells us that it was 'as Abraham worshipped that he grew strong in his faith, fully convinced that God was well able to fulfill all that He had promised'. What is wonderful is that the day started as any other. Nothing said that this was any different to any other. No hint, no indication, everything normal. Yet across the city a couple walk slowly towards his destiny and as he approaches the Temple the Spirit of God whispers to Simeon 'today'. After all those years of faithful waiting, of simply doing what God said to do 'today'.

Now it would be him, not a priest or a religious professional, who would take God Himself into his arms - and bless Him. In truth of course, that is always how we are a blessing to God. Not in the extraordinary moments of ministry, but in the quiet, unseen faithful daily routine. The book of Ruth perfectly illustrates this. Set mostly in Bethlehem it is 1/66th of the Bible. It tells the story of a foreign woman who simply lives her life in the ordinary. She marries, she is bereaved. She finds God in the midst and leaves her old way of life for one she doesn't know but which she has seen in others. It tells of her humility, it tells of her hard work, it speaks of her wisdom in seeking the advice of those older than her. It tells the love story of her marriage to Boaz. It points to the future as he redeems her from one 'who has more right to her'. It says nothing about miracles, it says nothing about powerfully preached sermons, it mentions nothing about important ministry. It ends with the birth of her son. A normal, ordinary life with it's highs and lows, filled mostly with neither. A life like Simeon's - a life perhaps like most of ours.

Yet look at the result. Ruth's son would himself have a son and he in turn would too. Obed had Jesse and Jesse had David. Out of Ruth God would bring the greatest King Israel would ever know. And out of David's line, in the town of Bethlehem would come a ruler far above even that. In the genealogy of Jesus, there stands Ruth - a foreigner, welcomed in by God's great hospitality.

Are you a younger person? Are you eager to 'get on' with life and ministry? Are you looking for the spectacular, bored with the ordinary? God is in the ordinary, Godliness is in the ordinary - if you don't find Him there, you won't find Him. Not in the earthquake, wind or fire - not in the spectacular. But in the still small voice of the ordinary.

Are you an older person? You feel passed by, that other's time has come, that ministry and significance have moved on. Not so in the Kingdom of God. Keep faithfully doing what you have learned of God, there is still eternity to build and you uniquely have the wisdom and the authority to see it established.

Are you somewhere in-between? Do the promises of God seem distant and receding? You're caught up in the everyday with little time for anything else - you see younger people and their

Part 3 - Refugees

energetic progress, you look ahead with some dread at an uncertain future. Keep faithfully doing what God has given you to do. Building the home, working hard, parenting your children - modeling the community of God. There will be times when you see God break through and with Simeon we shout to the world 'I have seen with my own eyes the salvation of my God'

Part 3 - Refugees

Notes:-

Part 3 - Refugees

Magi

Extract 27
The whole of Jerusalem is in turmoil, an embassy from some eastern country has arrived to speak to Herod. Israel hasn't had a state visit in living memory, not since the Romans took over. Even in Bethlehem there is speculation as to what it means. I'm not sure I care, I have exciting news of my own.

I am expecting Joseph's baby!

Extract 28
I should have cared. The ambassadors asked Herod where 'the one born to be King of the Jews' was. They asked Herod, that murdering pretend king, where the real king was! He must have been furious - rumour has it that he had his wife and own sons killed to protect his phony throne. Anyway, he pretended to want to know himself and he got the chief priests to look in the scriptures. I could have told him. 'And you Bethlehem, out of you will come a ruler'.

So they came. To our home, from the royal palace! As usual, Jesus was running around, scrapes on his knees and mud on his face. Chattering away as ever. They didn't mind though. When they saw him it was like the shepherds. They looked passed the toddler and met with Jesus. They bowed before him acknowledging his kingship. Then they solemnly presented him with gifts. It was funny watching these important men handing over presents to this bemused boy when Herod must have thought the gifts were for him! But what presents! Gold, incense, myrrh. A king, a priest and - well right now, I don't want to think about that.

Why would you give a small boy burial ointment?

Part 3 - Refugees

Extract 29

We've got to leave. The Magi have gone back without telling Herod about Jesus. He's sending the army to kill him. When will it end? I thought at last we could settle, be family.

Joseph's shouting, we must go.

Extract 30

I can hardly stop shaking. We've been in Egypt three days now. The escape was terrifying. Every moment I expected to hear hooves, shouts. What I heard instead was worse. Mother's screaming as Herod's murderers killed all the boys under two. We hid in a cave just outside the town. We heard it all. I wanted to go back to tell them to stop -better for us to die as a family than all those children. But Herod's men enjoy killing, they'd have killed us and all the others too.

I can't bear it. Some of Jesus' little friends, Benji, Sam, Nathan. I can't bear it.

Part 3 - Refugees

Behind the diary

Matthew 2:1-18

Back in the days of Daniel, the ruler of the known world took the brightest stars of the nations he had conquered and immersed them into Babylonian culture. He then appointed them as rulers under him of their home provinces but they also formed a cabinet acting as 'wise counsellors' helping the king rule in a way that was sensitive or at least understanding of the cultures he had taken over. They were known as 'Magi'. Now over 400 years later, Magi from the east (where Babylon was) come to Jerusalem. What an impact Daniel and his friends must have had! The aim was to immerse these Jews into Babylonian culture, instead they left a legacy which would last all these generations where people in what used to be Babylon were still looking for the signs that would mark the coming of Messiah. This is extraordinary. Instead of being conformed to the overwhelming pressures of that culture, they transformed enough of it that the memory lasted over 400 years! It survived the destruction of the empire, survived the new Roman influence and was dominant enough to allow this group to seek the new king.

What a challenge to us! Paul writes that we should not be conformed to this world but rather be transformed by the renewing of our mind. We are called not to become like the world but to see the world transformed into the Kingdom of God. This story shows us the influence that even a few can have on a whole society. Wesley would say 'give me 11 like minded men and we will turn this nation upside down'. He found them, and they did. So can we.

Part 3 - Refugees

Notes:-

Refugees

Extract 31
I've stopped shaking, but the tears will go on. 'Rachel weeping for her children, for they are no more'. And selfishly I keep asking; how much more running, how many more will want to kill my son, when can we be normal?

In calmer moments I reflect - our people spent 400 years trying to escape from Egypt into the Promised land. It was Joshua who took them the final steps. Now we have had to flee from the land, taking our Yeshua into Egypt.

Extract 32
Nazareth. Not exactly a warm welcome, but at least no stones. Somehow the stories of the shepherds, the royal visit and Herod's madness arrived before us (He finally died last month). I'm not saying that everyone believes us, but the open hostility is gone. Please God, time to settle, to re-build, to be a normal family.

Extract 33
I finally got to spend time with Father today. I brought Jesus and James to see their grand-parents. No-one knew quite what to say, them embarrassed at having been wrong to reject us so. Me, well, me because I'm not the 'me' that left.

I left my diary for them to read, it seemed the easiest way.

Extract 34
Daddy read my diary.

He came this morning. He brought me a new pen.

Part 3 - Refugees

Behind the Diary

Matthew 3:16-23

Incarnation is all about dislocation. Firstly Jesus must leave the Highest Heaven, He must lay aside power, knowledge and reach. Then He must relocate to the womb of a young girl. Next He will be born away from His 'home' town. And now this toddler will be uprooted twice more. Firstly as an asylum seeker into Egypt and then their return to Nazareth. Later Jesus would say 'foxes have holes and birds have nests, but the Son of Man has nowhere to lay his head'.

We are called to the role of incarnation - making Jesus present to a hostile world. As for Jesus, incarnation means dislocation. We are a people called to 'go' which as Loren Cunningham, the Founder of YWAM points out, means a change of location. A dis-location. Paul describes it as being in the world but not of it. The Children of Israel spent much time as nomads or exiles.

How at home are we in the world? Or are we living as citizens of heaven?

Childhood

Extract 35
I get so much less time to write nowadays. Five children and a husband make for a busy house! These last years have been wonderful - normal. Joseph's business growing, gradually being accepted by family and friends again. And of course seeing my children growing up! Jesus now seven down to Leah, just starting to walk.

But of course there are moments when the deeper reality breaks through, as in my heart I know it always will - and must. A couple of years ago, Jesus managed to open the cupboard where we keep the gifts from the Magi. He knows we often don't have much money, so when he saw the gold, he was naturally curious! We didn't say much - it really didn't seem the time.

Tomorrow is though - today he came home from school - he'd been in a fight with Reuben again. I was about to chastise him when he asked me what a bastard was. So, the whispers carry on and now we have to explain.

Extract 36
We've always told Jesus that he is special - but then what mother doesn't say that to her child? But there is something unique - not just about his birth, his father - but about him. The way he prays, the way he almost knows the scripture stories before they are finished - as if he's heard them before a long time ago. But above all, his goodness. Not that he isn't into everything like all boys his age, but there is nothing dark, nothing malicious. He's quick to apologise and very quick to praise and to love. I desperately want to protect him from the world that is so unlike him. But I know that is not why he has come to us.

And so we tell him. He nods at the circumstances of his conception and birth, he grins when we tell him of the first

Part 4 - Childhood

visitors. When we bring out the presents and give them to him, this time for real, he seems to understand. When I weep as I talk about Herod & Egypt, he comforts me. We spend hours talking about the scriptures, bringing what little understanding we can. At the end of it all, he stands by the window and says simply 'I see'.

Extract 37

As the eldest, Jesus spends more and more time with Joseph - learning the trade. Joseph is so patient with him! I remember the first time he got into the workshop, I was frantic. There he was by my feet, tripping me up as usual 'Off you go and play' I said - and off he went. When I looked for him a little later, I couldn't find him. I went down the street calling in at all my friends, but he wasn't there. Then Joseph came round the corner, carrying him. As Jesus saw me, he wriggled free and ran towards me shouting 'I helped dad build a boat!'. He went regularly after that, learning his trade, always something new! The time he wanted to hammer the nails himself. Joseph held the nails whilst Jesus tried to hit them. Jesus learned some new words and Joseph came home with bruised fingers! And the time he got sawdust in his eye. Such a small speck, so much hurt, so many tears.

But yesterday they brought me home a new box for my diary - they had made it together.

Soon there will be two carpenters in our house.

Part 4 - Childhood

Behind the Diary

There is no Biblical record of this period of Jesus' life, so these extracts are entirely imaginary. Yet there is a profound reality behind them. Jesus laid aside His rights to His Godly attributes (He could have exercised them at any point, but chose before the foundation of the world that He would not) and that includes His right to know all that is knowable. So He grows up as any other child, learning about His identity through His parents, through a growing understanding of scripture, through a relationship with His father that was unhindered by sin. He grows to believe the unbelievable - that He is the Son of God, that he is in fact equal with God. This is an extraordinary belief, but that is what it must remain - a belief. He could of course prove it beyond doubt by simply exercising His power, by reaching out for the knowledge that is His by right. But in proving it He will become utterly unlike that first Adam and therefore incapable of redeeming mankind.

Paul makes this point by describing Jesus as our 'last Adam'. First Adam was created in God's image, like God in character, but not of course in attributes. We don't need to be like God in power in order to relate to Him and to one another - we simply need to be like him in character, and that we were. But first Adam fell to temptation 'eat and be like God in attributes as well - you will have knowledge like God Himself'. The table below compares the two 'Adam's', see how Last Adam reverses the flaw of First Adam and thereby breaks open a way back. The death of first Adam and of all mankind since now has the potential for redemption as Last Adam is raised to life, so can we if we believe in Him and become like Him.

Part 4 - Childhood

First Adam	Last Adam
Like God in Character	Like God in Character
Not like God in attributes	Empties Himself of His Attributes
Not equal with God by right	Equal with God by right
Tempted to become like God	Tempted to exercise His Godly attributes
Grasped at the opportunity and died	Does not grasp at rights and is killed

This of course is the heart of the Gospel, but part of its price is simply this. Jesus had to live by faith. He could at any point have lived by sight, proving to all that He was what He believed Himself to be. But to do so would negate the possibility of salvation. For our sake he chooses to do what we must, live by faith.

Part 4 - Childhood

Learning Obedience

Extract 38

I'm writing now because I know I won't get chance tomorrow. I can hardly imagine where the time has gone! Jesus 12! No longer a growing boy but a young man in his own right. We're going to Jerusalem for the Passover to celebrate - I'm longing to go to the temple again - this time with Jesus - to feel the Father's presence, to be in the holy city again, to renew the reality of my call. And to see how Jesus responds to all of that in his own right.

Extract 39

Passover was wonderful! I always feel so close to God when we remember all he has done for us. But this year, all together as a family, Jesus taking part as a man, Leah asking the question 'Why this night, why this way?' and Joseph, inviting Jesus for the first time to tell us all why. It was as if he had been there! I could hear the breath in the horses nostrils, hear the ground shake under their hooves, feel the fear as they were pressed towards the water, see again the miracle as Moses struck the water. God rescuing his people. As I looked at him as he told it I could see him change. No longer a boy eagerly retelling a well known story. But a man, a teacher with wisdom and authority far beyond his years. At the end Joseph put his arm round him and nodded. 'Well done son, I'm proud of you'.

Extract 40

How quickly good times turn to bad. We've just spent the last three days looking for Jesus. For three days I felt I had lost him. At first we thought he was traveling back with friends. By the time we felt the need to look it took a day to retrace our steps. Every moment I was afraid we'd come across someone who would tell us the worst - robbers, slave-traders. But nothing, no sign. When we got back to Jerusalem we went to everyone we knew, but no-one knew anything. Finally we went to the temple to pray for a miracle - and there I suppose it was. Jesus, debating with

Part 4 - Childhood

the teachers of the law - asking them questions as if he were the teacher and they the disciples. And they were responding, nodding at the quality of his questions, taking him seriously. If we hadn't been so angry, so distressed it would have been a precious moment. When he saw us, he finished his question then came over to us as if nothing was wrong. Joseph was furious on my behalf, but when challenged, Jesus was surprised and at once apologetic. We sat down and he explained. 'For years you have pointed me to the scriptures, told me the stories. You know that I am called to bring good news to the poor. You, mother, you know who I am better than anyone. Surely you knew that once I became a man in my own right, I would need to be about my Father's business?'

As he said those words I felt Simeon's sword pierce my heart a little. Not just for myself at the thought of my son moving on, but for Joseph too. His natural hopes that Jesus would take over from him. And those words, innocently spoken but how they must have hurt 'My Father's business'. Yet Joseph was God's choice as well and instead of a bitter reply borne out of disappointment, Joseph said 'Indeed you must, it is what we have given ourselves for Jesus. It is what we have suffered to bring about. But not yet, not like this. Up till now you have been obedient to us because it was your duty as a child to his parents. Now you need to learn to be obedient out of choice, out of love. Then you will be ready to fulfill all our Father has for you.' Jesus looked at Joseph and a broad smile lit his face. 'You're right' he said 'thank you!' Without looking back he said simply. 'Two carpenters in Nazareth then' and with that he swung Leah to his shoulders and marched off towards home.

Part 4 - Childhood

Behind the Diary

Luke 2: 40-52

There is a lot of confusion about sin! Fundamentally it is about broken relationship, not broken rules, it is about being right with God, not about being right. Before Jesus is 12 He is regarded by the religious and legal code as a boy - not responsible for His own decisions, subject in all things to His parents. Their choices were His choices, what they said, He must do. His obedience up to that point was not a freely chosen obedience, but a mandatory one. Now He becomes a man in His own right, capable and responsible for His own choices, no longer under the legal jurisdiction of Mary & Joseph. Immediately He begins to do what He thinks is a fulfilling of His call. 'Did you not know that I must be about my Father's business?'

But salvation really hinges on genuine moral choice. The triune God chose freely to go ahead with creation, The Son freely chose that He would become man and suffer the consequences, the Holy Spirit freely chose that He would dwell in the lives of sinful people, the Father freely chose to withold His hand when His Son is crucified.... But up till this point in Jesus earthly life, He has not exercised choice in His own right, He hasn't learned obedience that is freely given rather than a legal requirement. And scripture tells us that after the conversation with His wise parents, he returns home an 'learns obedience'. An obedience that one day Paul tells us would lead to death on a cross. Is it possible that Jesus, in faith, but in human immaturity, in the zeal of youth, got the timing wrong? It isn't sin, it's simply getting something wrong. Let's take this example, let's be people willing and ready to take faith risks, it's not sin if we get it wrong from time to time. The key is to act and be quick to learn obedience.

Part 4 - Childhood

Notes:-

Part 4 - Childhood

One carpenter

Extract 41
And now one. The fever came and took him quickly. So strong - my strength for these 20 years. But no longer. Part of me died with him. My Joseph, my kind, strong carpenter. How quickly time goes, how frail and fleeting we are - it seems only a moment since that first day and now, here I am, not an eager girl, but a widow. Only one carpenter in Nazareth today.

Behind the Diary

There is no record of Joseph's death, just the inference of it from the absence of any mention of this key figure after the visit to Jerusalem when Jesus is 12. The timing is significant. Jesus now a man had the right to leave home, but chooses, after discussion with His parents, to return and 'learn obedience'. Eighteen years between Him first setting out to begin ministry and it actually happening. One of the key things he would learn is that sometimes the big picture has to wait for the sake of the individual. Uniquely, God has both in view all the time. The needs of the many, the needs of the one. In the future a woman who needed restoring whilst a ruler waits, another woman who needed comfort whilst the world waited for news of resurrection. Now a family that needs His support whilst the plan of salvation waits until 'the time is fully come'.

How patient are we? Do we give equal attention to the one or two that God brings across our path or are we impatient to get on with the 'important' big picture, more obvious ministry? We are created for relationship, to love and be loved. The truth is, unless we learn this and act out of it, any other 'ministry' will be dead, dry, fruitless - just so much busy-ness and wasted energy.

On the other hand, let take great confidence from the reality that God is as focused and committed to the individual as He is to the course of nations, 'to the upholding of the universe by his word of power.'

Part 5 - Messiah

John

Extract 42
Elizabeth has been so supportive over these last few years. Jesus has taken on the role of head of house, but the visits of my dear cousin are precious. She's had her own troubles of course- Zechariah died the same year as Joseph, but now John has left home too. She is so worried for him. He should have been a priest, but they both knew that God had a different plan, so they declared him a Nazarite -dedicated to God from birth. All of which was fine, but he seems to have gone wild! We know him well but he scares me a little - his hair, his clothes, but above all his absolute unbending zeal for God - it's hard to explain - I first saw it in Abel and I've always recognised it in Jesus. And now, increasingly in myself. It's the strength that comes from knowing God and resolutely following his word. Maybe we're all like Abel - all builders in God's kingdom - with a few scars collected along the way.

Extract 43
Anyway, he's gone – down by the Jordan, living wild, looking wild. The people love him – there's the usual rumour that maybe he's the Messiah – he's quick to deny that but there's no denying that something special is happening down there. I went with Elizabeth, we just stayed on the edge of the crowd and watched. It's amazing, people from every walk of life, business people mixing with fishermen, money-changers with some of the religious leaders. All listening to the same message of hope. That the kingdom is at hand!

John stands there shouting out 'Prepare the way of the Lord, change your lives, get ready for the king who is coming'. Of course most people would love to have more control of their lives – see the Roman's kicked out, the chains of the law loosened a bit, some basic justice. No wonder they love him! But the authorities feel threatened and that's dangerous. Whilst we were

Part 5 - Messiah

there some Scribes came down, pretending to be interested, but John saw straight through them. He shouted at them 'Who warned you, you brood of vipers, go and change your lives, then come back'. The crowd cheered and they slunk away, the crowd saw it as a victory and cheered all the more. Elizabeth and I know differently.

Oh God, why can't your people see?

Behind the diary

Luke 3 1-17

I spent many years as a young Christian wondering about this. Every time Jesus talked about good news, He declared it to be that 'the kingodom of God is at hand'. And as the forerunner of Jesus, John brings the same message. Yet in what way is 'the kingdom of God' good news? My sins forgiven, guilt dealt with, a hope for the future, salvation - all these sounded like good news, yet this isn't what John or Jesus point to. They say that the good news is that the Kingdom of God is breaking in to the world.

The truth is that we have made a divide between the physical and the spiritual that simply does not exist. My old understanding of good news was overly spiritualised, but God wants to relate to a whole person - shalom. So His good news encompasses every aspect of life for the whole of life. It addresses the provision of physical needs; healing, health, food, shelter, clothing, rest. It addresses emotional needs; peace, joy, comfort, adventure, security, identity, significance, love. It addresses the past; healing, forgiveness, perspective. It addresses the future; hope, justice, celebration, eternity. And it brings the reality of all these into the now through the dynamic of a restored, living relationship with God Himself.

This is the good news we have, this is the good news we share. The Kingdom of God is at hand!

Part 5 - Messiah

Notes:-

Part 5 - Messiah

Baptism

Extract 44
Things are changing again. At least I recognise the signs now. Jesus has his brothers doing more of the day to day running of the business. John is gathering larger crowds and annoying more people with his preaching. But Herod is getting stronger too. He's already taken control of two provinces and had the Romans appoint him king. Now, not satisfied with stealing his brother's territory, he's stolen his wife. I know he cares little for our traditions and less still for God, but this is dangerous – the people are incensed. And John is right in the middle of it. Not content with upsetting our leaders, he's now railing against Herod, prophesying against him – more and more the people see him as a rallying point, as a political leader. I'm frightened for him. And for Jesus. He went today.

I'd seen it coming but it's still so hard to let go. It feels like I've lost so much already – I'm his mother, I want to protect, to build home, to shelter. But I think back to that first night, when Gabriel stood there, full of authority and God's power – waiting for a young girl to give her permission. So I've learned this about love. It doesn't cling, it doesn't insist on its own way, it sets free, it trusts. But it still hurts.

Extract 45
I went with him as far as the Jordan. John was there of course, along with the usual crowds and a cohort of the palace guard – keeping an eye on things. As we began to move through the crowd John seemed to know we were there. For a long moment time seemed to stop and slowly the crowds turned their heads towards us. Then with a deep sigh John spoke. 'Behold. The Lamb of God who takes away the sin of the world'. Then he pointed at Jesus. 'This is the one I keep telling you about. The one whose sandal I am unworthy to untie. The one.' The crowd held its breath, then Jesus broke the spell - with a huge smile on

his face he splashed into the water and clapped John on the back. 'It's time. I've come to be baptised'. John was horrified. 'I need to be baptised by you, not you by me!'. But Jesus laughed and shook his head. 'Let's fulfill the law John, this baptism of yours, it's about making right choices – right? So we can do this can't we?'. As the light dawned, John nodded again and together with Jesus walked deeper into the river. Then he put his big arms around my son and baptised him.

The crowd must have seen it a hundred times that week. Declaring afresh your trust in God, committing yourself to walk a different path, pleading with God to cleanse you with more than water. But as Jesus was plunged beneath the water it seemed so much more. My heart stopped. It looked for a moment as if he was gone. Not a washing, but a burial. I think the crowd felt something too, there was an extraordinary hush – a collective holding of breath. Then just as suddenly, the water broke and Jesus shook his hair, spraying droplets everywhere. We all let out a gasp and out of nowhere a dove hovered over Jesus before resting on his shoulder. It looked for all the world as Noah's dove must have done when for the first time it found dry land.

Once more God's Spirit has found a place to rest.

Extract 46

As we watched in awe with a supernatural silence all around, a voice spoke – it seemed to reverberate off the hills – 'This is my son, in whom I am well pleased'. Jesus turned his head and looked into my eyes. My son. His Father. Then he was gone, without a word, striding out into the wilderness. I remembered Joseph's words all those years ago at Passover. 'I'm proud of you'. Jesus left us then when he was 12, but the time wasn't right and he came back with us. This is different, now the time has fully come and I know he isn't coming back. I began to cry then I felt a hand on my shoulder. James, strong, resolute James. 'Come home mother'. And so I went, leaving some of my heart behind.

Part 5 - Messiah

Behind the Diary

Luke 3: 10-22

From this point forward, Jesus begins to preach and to establish the Kingdom. 'For this purpose' John would write 'was the Son of God revealed, to destroy all the works of the evil one'. And now He begins to fulfill this. The lepers will be cleansed, the blind will receive their sight, the oppressed will find freedom, the accused will find acceptance rather than condemnation, the lame will walk, the people will be fed and the dead will be raised. And time and time again the people and leaders will ask 'by what authority do you do these things?' It's a profound question.

The answer lies in the events in this passage. Up until this point, Jesus, though fully God by right, has done nothing miraculous. He has persistently chosen in accordance with that choice made before the foundation of the world, that He would be 'last Adam'. Coming to this earth, not 'counting equality with God as something to be grasped' but 'emptying Himself...' In short, choosing to be like that first Adam - like God in character, but by choice, not acting like him in attributes. And in the profound drama of baptism, He declares this to all who will understand. He identifies Himself with humanity. He shouts 'I am come like that first Adam' and though He personally needs no cleansing, demonstrates the depth of His humility by this act. Jesus' baptism is a profound declaration of this truth. The Messiah, though he has every right to act as God, will not. He will to the end persist in this humble choice, to be like first Adam so that he can restore us to the heights of heaven.

But now filled with that other member of the triune family, He begins to perform the miraculous. By whose power? It's clear. By the power of the Holy Spirit. 'Not by might, not by power, but by my Spirit, says the Lord'. So now we have it. Last Adam comes, like God in character, choosing to be like humanity in attributes. Living by faith not by sight, filled with the Spirit, He begins to

Part 5 - Messiah

establish the Kingdom in power. What a model, what a challenge. Are we not re-created in God's image - like Him in character but not in attributes? Are we not called and enabled to live by faith and not by sight? Are we not commanded to 'be being filled with the Spirit'? Are we not then called, as His body, to also bear the fruit of the Spirit and exercise the gifts of the Spirit - just as he did, in order to establish the kingdom in power? No wonder Jesus would one day say to those like us 'greater things than these will you do...'

Part 5 - Messiah

Synagogue

Extract 47

It's been three months since his baptism. Three months since we saw him. We've heard lots of rumours – that he's joined the Essene community out in the desert, that he'd gone mad – fasting for 40 days, that angels have taken him away, of amazing miracles in Capernaum. I suppose one day he will tell us. All I know for now is that yesterday he came home! There we were, Leah and me preparing for Sabbath and there he was. As if he had never been away – the smiles, the greetings, the questions to the boys about the business. But for everything that is the same there is something that is different. The same smile and laugh, but with a different glint in his eye. The same kind strength but with a resolve that scares me. I love my son, I know him so well. But who is this that has come home? My Jesus and yet more than my Jesus. My son and yet so much more than my son.

Anyway, I don't know how long he will be here, but I'm determined to enjoy every minute!

Extract 48

We went to synagogue together. As we entered the attendant handed Jesus the scroll. I guess everyone wanted to know what had happened and this gave Jesus the chance to speak. When the moment came everyone was quiet. He stood and read from Isaiah. 'The Spirit of Lord is upon me, for he has anointed me'. As he spoke it seemed to me not to be a reading from some long dead prophet but a simple statement of fact. Of course it's a famous passage, everyone loves the hope it brings. But equally everyone is fed up hearing inspirational sermons that come to nothing or political speeches that end in riots or worse. When he finished reading we all held our breath to see which it would be. Slowly Jesus sat down and then in a quiet voice that I could hardly hear he simply said this. 'Today, in your hearing this scripture is fulfilled'. For a moment we waited for him to

Part 5 - Messiah

continue. Then we realised that he was the sermon. He meant that he was anointed by the spirit to preach good news to the poor, to proclaim the year of the Lord's favour, to bind up the broken hearted. Of course, many of them had seen the Spirit come to him when he was baptised, so there was much agreeing as they understood his words. I was so excited, the people who had so often rejected my son, were openly approving. But of course we all wanted to know what it meant, where he had been, whether the rumours were true. So he started. 'You've heard rumours about mighty works? Well, why did I not do them here? Because you think you know me, but you don't. "A prophet is not without honour, except in his own country". But God has always been for all nations – that's why Elijah was sent to a widow from Nain'. I didn't hear the rest, I could see the approval drain away, the old hostilities rise. 'Who are you to instruct us? We know you; you're only a carpenter – Joseph's son – and maybe not even that'. As Jesus continued to chastise us for our lack of commitment to God's plan – that we should be a blessing to the nations, the anger rose. Eventually a crowd of the men took hold of Jesus and wrestled him out of the synagogue. We tried desperately to intervene, but they were wild, racing off with Jesus up the hill. I felt so helpless, my son and I can do nothing but watch as they half drag him to a place where they can kill him. After a few moments they were out of sight then suddenly, just as I was dreading hearing the worst, back came Jesus, simply walking through the crowd, unharmed, with every impression of being in control of the situation.

I'm not sure what frightened me most, the crowd's reaction or the authority that seems to rest on Jesus.

Behind the Diary

Luke 4

So, Jesus, filled with the Spirit is led by the Spirit. It's a simple truth, if we want to be led by God, we need to be filled by God. If we want to be filled by God we must be willing to be led by God... But look where He leads - after 18 years of waiting from the age of twelve till this point, He is led not inot ministry, but into the wilderness. 'The wisdom of God is wiser than the wisdom of the wisest men'. Household decisions, business decisions, relationship decisions - all need the wisdom of God! And He is eager to give it, if we are eager to receive it... Of course we are created with intelligence and the capability to evaluate and draw conclusions. Of course God can use these and our experience and that of other Godly people to lead and guide. But often the rational or the emotional is all that we use. We exclude God's wisdom, simply praying after we have concluded, that God will bless our decision. Rather we should seek God, exercise the gifts and use the information from all of these to inform our final decision.

So Jesus enters the desert and encounters the enemy. Remember, Jesus is here as Last Adam, refusing to exercise His rights as God. He therefore believes that he is God, but the only way He could know that it was true for sure would be to exercise His rights as God - the very thing He has comitted not to do. It is no surprise then that the enemy attacks this point of vulnerability. Three times he demands: 'If you are the son of God...' and each time invites Jesus to prove it by exercising some aspect of His rights as God. To feed Himself by the miraculous, to see God fulfil scripture in His defence, to oversee the whole earth at once. Omnipotence, omniscience, omnipresence - the very attributes of God - do these and prove it, don't live by faith, you could know for sure. Think how much easier it would all be then! But each time Jesus refuses to because he knows the scriptures point to a different route.

Part 5 - Messiah

Notice too that first Adam meets the enemy in a place of abundance - the garden of Eden. Jesus meets him in a place of death and barrenness. First Adam is tempted to be like God in attributes - to which he had neither need nor right. Here, the enemy tests Last Adam in the same way, to be like God in attributes - to which He has absolute right - but which He has in humility emptied Himself of, in order to become like us.

And in this most extreme of tests, Jesus remains resolute. Not because He knows, but because he stands firm in faith. As a result, the scripture says that He comes out of the wilderness in the power of the Spirit. Filled, led, tested, empowered. Should we not expect the same pattern in our own lives? John warned us didn't he? 'He will baptise you with the Spirit and with fire'. There must be refining, testing - if Jesus, already pure, experiences this, how much more must we?

Finally, as He comes to fulfill the specific call there is one more step. 'The Spirit of the Lord has anointed me'

Part 5 - Messiah

Wedding

Extract 49
I love weddings! Maybe it's because I never had a proper one, maybe this time I'm so excited because Jesus will be there. Joanna, one of our cousins from Cana has a daughter getting married and we've all been invited. Jesus has to attend as head of our household – not that I care why, I haven't seen him since that dreadful day at the Synagogue, it will be nice to relax and celebrate again. Of course he won't be there alone. He seems to have gathered a strange group of friends, from what I hear, they're not the sort of group you'd choose to have at a party. Tax Collectors are bad news at any time, not exactly guaranteed to bring joy to a party! But I'm most worried about the Zealots in the group. They're basically terrorists hiding behind a political party. They scare me – I just hope there won't be any trouble.

Extract 50
There was trouble, but not the sort I had feared. On the third day of the party, they ran out of wine. Maybe Jesus' friends drank more than planned, maybe there were just more people because of the 12 of them. Whatever, the wine ran out. Joanna was desperate, the shame was too much for her. I knew what it was like not to be offered hospitality, I knew what it was like to have your dreams of a proper wedding shattered by shame. I couldn't stand it. I went to Jesus and explained the problem. He wrestled with it – he said 'it's not my time' – he thought I'd understand that, it's what we had told him when he was 12. But if it's time to leave home, if it's time to begin ministry, it's time to start replacing shame with honour.

My eyes pleaded. Still he hesitated. 'What's this to do with me' he tried. I wanted to scream 'everything', it's got everything to do with you. Do you know how I longed for a proper wedding instead of a quick prayer? Do you know how much I long for your wedding, knowing there won't be one? Do you know what it feels

Part 5 - Messiah

like to have your friends and family ashamed of you? I can't bear any more – do something! My voice remained silent, but my eyes blazed. Tears began to fill Jesus eyes, he put his hand on my shoulder and nodded. I turned and told the servants to do whatever he said.

Extract 51

I don't know what I expected him to do. I'm not even sure what he did. The next I heard the chief steward was shouting for everyone's attention. Poor Joanna, she must have thought he had discovered there was no more wine – she had seen a servant taking him a cup of water. He banged the cup on the table and said 'At ordinary parties, they serve the best wine at the beginning then when everyone's too drunk to notice they serve up what might as well be water.' I thought Joanna was going to faint and my own heart sank. But before I could go to help, he carried on 'but in this great house, your hospitality knows no bounds - you've saved the best wine till last'. There was clapping and cheering, and a great deal more drinking. I looked at Joanna, happier and taller than I'd ever seen her before, I saw her daughter with her new husband laughing and dancing. And then I saw Jesus. He'd been watching me the whole time. He had that twinkle in his eye and a gentle smile on his face. He walked across the room and as he passed by he whispered:

'New wine. New wineskins. A surprising celebration on the third day.

You're right, it has everything to do with me'

Part 5 - Messiah

Behind the Diary

John 2: 1-12

Luke we know from what he writes sets out to record 'an orderly account'. John, writing many years later has a different purpose. His ordering of events is to do with importance not sequence. He describes John the Baptist as 'the greatest of the prophets' meaning the last in line, the ultimate old covenant prophet. Now, in a similar vein he tells this wonderful story describing it as 'the first of the signs'. Not in sequence necessarily, but in importance. My guess is that we wouldn't naturally view it in this way. It isn't as profound as the blind receiving sight nor as dramatic as the feeding of the five thousand. Yet John is right. This miracle embodies the heart of the gospel, the heart of what God has come to accomplish and sets the context for everything else. We are designed for welcome into the heart of a loving triune God. Hospitality is at the heart of love, and love is at the heart of who God is. Yet we have made the world inhospitable and we have become inhospitable - as dramatically witnessed at Jesus own birth. We were designed for celebration and enjoyment, yet sin has diminished this to occasional pleasure in the midst of a life often characterised by struggle.

In that context, Jesus comes to Cana and to a wedding. Marriage is the ultimate picture of the relationship God longs for us to enjoy with Him. Above all else it should be a joy filled occasion representing the highest hospitality - a man and woman inviting the other into the very heart of their lives. A hospitality echoed by the friends and family invited to witness and celebrate this great occasion. Yet as with our lives, shame threatens to invade and despoil. In place of abundant hospitality, the wine runs out. Who can redeem this situation? Who can restore the possibility of true hospitality, who can open for us a door into the heart of God, who can turn shame into celebration? Jesus! On the third day, the wine, the representation of life and joy, begins to flow again. 'This, the greatest of the signs, Jesus did in Cana'.

Part 5 - Messiah

Notes:-

Part 5 - Messiah

Goodbye

Extract 52
I have to go to Elizabeth, there's terrible news. Herod's had John in prison for weeks now – we'd almost got used to it. Herod's wife was behind it of course, she couldn't stand John stirring up the people against her relationship with her husbands' brother. But we thought it was just to teach John a lesson. We thought that after a few weeks he would be released with a warning. We were hoping that he'd feel he'd made his point and settle down a bit. Jesus tried to warn us all, he sent a message to John using the same reading from Isaiah that he preached on in our synagogue. We saw it as an encouragement, I suppose we heard what we wanted. 'The blind will see, the lame walk, joy for those who mourn, garlands of praise, the anointing Spirit of God. But the message wasn't in what he said but in what he missed out. The prisoners being set free.

Yesterday, John was beheaded.

Extract 53
Thirty years ago I made this journey with fear and excitement in my heart. Gabriel had told me that Elizabeth was pregnant – after all those years of waiting, hope and faith had been fulfilled. Then, Elizabeth's condition confirmed my own. Now I have come again and I fear that Elizabeth's loss will all too soon confirm my own.

I have no words that can console, only more tears.

Part 5 - Messiah

Behind the Diary

Matthew 14: 1-12

The Herod in this passage is not the same as the one at the start of Jesus' life. Following the death of that Herod ('Herod the Great') the territory was split into three and 'tetrarch's appointed by Rome to govern. This Herod was politically astute and gradually gained control over one of the other regions, quelling what was to the Romans, a very troublesome area. On the back of this success, Herod travelled to Rome to seek an audience with the Emperor who, at Herod's request, granted him the honorary title 'King'. Later, Jesus would tell a political parable 'once there was a man who went to ask for a kingdom'. Like John, He made no effort to avoid trouble. he would mock Herod's self agrandisment, He would tell Nicodemus to get a life, He too would describe some as 'white-washed tombs'. Yet He was never strident or judgmental. Where people responded to Him - whatever their rank, His heart was warm, His spirit welcoming.

We live in a world where a great deal of energy goes into deriding others. Ultimately we feel better at other's expense - often they have no recourse, no opportunity to provide a context - we simply ridicule. At other times 'the church' has attempted to have a prophetic voice but has so often ended up self-promoting or sounding holier-than-thou. The power and credibility with which Jesus spoke into these situations rested on His unimpeachable character and His humilty. When He denounced leaders it was not because He wanted to replace them - far from it, He would submit to them even to death. When he chastised it was not out of some similar fault in His own life that He was somehow blind to, it was rooted in a desire, not for personal gain, but that those He was chastising might know the truth and respond to His grace.

How can we be as fearless in speaking truth? How can we be as humble as we speak it?

Part 5 - Messiah

Picnic

Extract 54
With John gone, Jesus seems to be more prominent. The crowds that used to go to John, now follow my son. Everyone wants to know - was John a prophet, was he Elijah, was he the Messiah? There seem to be more questions in his death than when he was alive. We went into the hills yesterday to be with Jesus. It was extraordinary. People from all the villages had come, thousands of us, all there to hear what answer Jesus would give. He astounded us. 'John was the last prophet of the old covenant'. What did he mean, there's only one covenant? He had us spellbound. So many stories, so much humour, so much from his childhood. 'If your friend has a plank in his eye, take the speck out of your own first', 'if you're building a house, don't build it on sand!', 'look at the flowers, not even Solomon was dressed like these'.

Extract 55
None of us wanted to go back to the ordinariness of our lives. We wanted to stay in his presence, to feel the warmth of his words, bathe in the love of God. By the time any of us realised, it was too late for many families to get home and prepare a meal. Some of Jesus friends started to argue, one of them urged Jesus to send us all home but I could see that look in Jesus eye. 'I've fed them all day, you feed them now'. Most of them panicked, trying to work out how much it would cost, where they could buy food, what they already had and how many it would feed. It was so funny, I could see Jesus looking, hoping to see faith in return. And he found it. Not in any of his friends, but in a small boy – he ran up to Jesus and offered him his lunch – a couple of small fish and a piece of bread. It was a precious moment, we didn't know whether to laugh or cry! Jesus friends weren't impressed though, they dismissed him crossly. Jesus became angry, not at the boy, but his disciples. 'Never stop children coming to me, he's come to me with what he has, he's come to me with faith' What happened

Part 5 - Messiah

next will live with us all forever. Jesus took the food and gave thanks to God then he began to divide it and pass it out to us all. It just kept coming. Everyone got fed and the food kept coming. In the end we gathered up baskets full of food left over after everyone was full. At first we just enjoyed the food and then we began to understand what was happening. The last person to feed the people with food from nowhere was Moses. The man who saved his people.

Part 5 - Messiah

Behind the Diary

Luke 9: 10-17

In saying to the disciples 'you feed them' Jesus sets up the classic problem we so often face. The resources we have are just not adequate to the task. From the everyday problem of making ends meet as a family to world issues such as poverty, war, disease, global warming.... it seems beyond us at every level. Human ingenuity, trying harder - nothing is anything like enough, the problem is still there or worsening. Aid agencies speak of 'compassion fatigue', people get fed up of seeing the same problem and overwhelmed feel helpless and for their own sanity, withdraw. God never does that. His love 'endures all things, bears all things, hopes all things'. Faced with the exhaustion of our effort and capability we finally look beyond our self to the one whose capacity and resources are infinite. We are so wired to doing it ourselves, to self-reliance, to trying to control - pride in short, that we rarely turn to God until it all but too late.

Yet Jesus Himself says that God knows our needs before we articulate them. So why doesn't God just provide - given that He knows too well our reluctance to ask? Why do we need to ask, to pray, to cry out? Doesn't it seem perverse that an all-knowing God should wait till we tell Him what He already knows before He acts? Jesus asks 'what have you got?' in order to face them with the reality of the answer: 'Not enough'. He doesn't do it to criticise 'well why not, that's bad planning'. He doesn't do it to humiliate. He simply gets them to the place where they realise that they can't do it by themselves. Then He invites them to bring what they have and trust Him for the rest. That's what it's all about. A genuine partnership between God and His people. Founded on an intimate, trusting relationship. He's our Father, our friend, our helper. The plan is always to recognise that there are things we don't know, things we can't do, things we don't have - and recognising that, we go to the one who loves us, acknowledging what we have, what we don't have and trusting that together we will have all we need. Without the loaves and fishes there would be nothing to multiply. Without God there would only be enough for one.

Come to the God who loves you and get Him involved in the those things where you don't have enough - more and more you'll realise that means the whole of your life.

Part 5 - Messiah

Threat

Extract 56
News of the miracle spread quickly. No-one thinks of him as my son anymore, everyone wants to claim him as theirs. Everyone has an opinion about who he is, what he should do, whose side he is on. Everyone thinks they own him. It's so dangerous. He offends our own religious leaders yet some of them openly follow him. Even the wife of Herod's Chief of Staff supports his work. Already there are rumours that the Romans are fearful of his influence. They've put down so many rebellions, killed so many 'Christs'. In truth, I'm frightened for him. They killed John, if they could find a way, I'm afraid they'll kill my son.

Extract 57
I couldn't stand it anymore, I told James and the boys to come with me, to reason with him, help him understand that the way he is going will get him killed. But when we got to where he was I was shocked, the crowd was larger than I had ever seen – it seemed as if the whole of Israel was listening to my son. Jesus looked exhausted, we tried to push our way through, but we couldn't get to him. In the end we passed a message from hand to hand pleading with him to come home. When he heard received the message he looked up and sadly shook his head. 'My mother and my brothers are those who understand God's word and allow me to fulfill it'. Our eyes met and my heart broke one more time.

Extract 58
We stayed a while, to watch, to listen. But soon, Jesus and his disciples moved towards the lake and got into a boat. We all followed hoping that he would preach from the boat so that more people could hear. But not this time, he really was exhausted and as soon as they were ready, Jesus lay down in the back of the boat and the fishermen in his group set sail. The crowd gradually turned away, realising the show was over. But as we were leaving someone shouted 'Look over there!' We turned and

Part 5 - Messiah

my heart stopped. The sky over the lake had darkened, a howling storm was sweeping towards the boat. I know lakes, I know storms and I had never seen anything like this. We stood transfixed as the storm hit the boat. They had almost no time to do anything. It was far from the shore now – almost half way to Gerasa. We saw the sail come down and the boat turn towards the waves. It didn't seem anything like enough. Time and again we saw it swamped by waves, almost overturned, and with each wave the boat sank a little more. Minutes ago I had tried to save Jesus from men, now it seemed the very powers of hell had been unleashed. And then it stopped. Not gradually, not a normal abating of wind and waves. It just stopped. And there standing in the prow was Jesus. He's my son, but who is he?

Part 5 - Messiah

Behind the Diary

Luke 8: 19-25

If we understand this story we will understand life! All that most people, most of the time, have to act on is what they can grasp with their five senses. Reality is what we can touch, see, hear, taste, smell. We take all of that, see how it makes us feel, work out what it means on the basis of reason and experience, then make a decision. It's absurd, it ignores the biggest part of life entirely! It takes no account of the spiritual realm which is eternal, but focuses on this minute physical aspect as if that is all there is! We're worse off than someone walking round with their eyes shut. Always tripping over stuff, bumping into things. Getting hurt and bruised on the furniture of life... and wondering why, trying to make sense of it, but with no hope of doing so till we open our eyes... Jesus has just spent days teaching the crowds this truth. 'Your Father in heaven knows you need these things - but life consists of more than the physical needs....'

Note where the Father is - in the heavenly realm (as Jesus again stresses in His model prayer: 'Our Father in heaven'). Paul points out why: 'our battle is not against flesh and blood' - ie the physical world 'but against the principalities and powers *in the heavenly realm*'. ie where the Father is! He has placed Himself, for our sake at the heart of the battle. He is right where He can be most effective on our behalf.

But most of the time, we don't even notice the battle. We just need something to eat, somewhere to live, a secure job, a better car, a nicer spouse... We're not even alert to the strings that the enemy is pulling; we think we are in control, criminally unaware of the part we are unconsciously playing in the wider war... This life is both physical and spiritual. We need the Spirit of God to gift us with spiritual eyes and ears so that we can discern it as clearly as we do the physical realm.

So what is the full picture in this story? Jesus is God, Jesus has

Part 5 - Messiah

spoken, Jesus is with them. They have God's word 'let us go to the other side of the lake'. They have God's presence. But half way across, a storm appears. Many of the disciples are fishermen - experts with boats, knowledgeable about storms. And so like us, they get sucked in to thinking that this is all there is. When the storm hits, they do all you do when a storm hits. But it isn't enough - just like the loaves and fishes weren't enough. So they wake Jesus to let Him know that He is about to die. They have no hope, they've done all you can do and they can't see beyond the physical. They don't look to the fact that God is with them. They don't rest on the reality that God has spoken about the outcome. They look at the physical reality and ignore the bigger, greater reality in which lies the answer. So Jesus does for them what they should have done themselves. He rebukes the wind and waves.

Now why would you do that? Wind and waves are inanimate - there's no point being angry with them, futile surely to tell them off for drowning you... Yet that's what Jesus does and with surprising results. They abate and all is calm. But of course Jesus is not actually addressing wind and wave - life is more than the physical. Why are they crossing the lake? Who is there? A man whose life is tormented by the demonic. What is Jesus intent in crossing the lake? To set him free. If now we look at the bigger picture, the one that includes the spiritual realm as well as the physical, what seems random, obscure comes sharply into focus. Jesus comes to 'destroy all the works of the evil one'. The demons discern the closing presence of the Son of God. They fear Him and want to prevent Him freeing this man and perhaps unmaking them. What now do we think is the source of the storm? Is it simply a physical event? Or is it provoked by the demonic? If the disciples had stood back from their cleverness with boats for a moment and exercised spiritual discernment, might they not of understood the source and acted accordingly? Might they too not have rebuked the enemy - resisting them that they must flee? Jesus comes to the man and sets him free. Free to live, to witness, to enjoy life in all its fullness. The demons

Part 5 - Messiah

end up in a herd of pigs that they cannot control and end up being drowned. That's how the battle works. We discern what the enemy is seeking to do, and as we stand firm, the very strategy that the enemy purposed against us becomes that which defeats him. The demons sought to drown Jesus and the disciples, in the end they were the ones that experienced drowning.

Some I know will respond that we can go too far - that we see demons under every chair and behind every bad event. That's not the biggest danger here. The biggest danger is that we remain completely ignorant of the real world, ineffective in it whilst damaging ourselves and others in the process. What we need is for the body of Christ to collectively exercise the gifts of the Spirit to effectively discern the full reality of what is going on and act accordingly. Is it a natural event? Is it human folly? Is it demonic activity? It could be any or a combination of all, but if we don't open our spiritual eyes we will never know and never be able to respond appropriately. But there's one thing more: God doesn't give all the spiritual senses to one person, He shares them round His people. It means you can't do this discernment on your own. If you're going to be effective at understanding the big picture, you're going to need to trust others and everyone is going to have to play their part.

It's called church, and against this, not even the very gates of hell can prevail.

Part 5 - Messiah

Notes:-

Jairus

Extract 59
It wasn't over then. A short while later news spread that Jesus had freed a demonised man in Gerasa and that they were all on their way back. By the time they returned, the crowd was even bigger than in the morning. As the disciples and Jesus got out of the boat they were immediately swallowed by the crowd. I feared then that he would be crushed, so many people pressing against him. Then there was a cry from the far side of the crowd and incredibly a path was made. We realised it must be someone of importance and someone recognised him – it was Jairus the ruler of the local Synagogue. Immediately my mind went back to that moment in our synagogue. The crowd kept me from my son, it didn't help when the Synagogue leaders wanted to kill him but now they parted to make way for this one. But my anger melted when I heard his story. His 12 year old daughter was dying. They'd tried everything, spent everything and now he was humbling himself before Jesus, pleading for him to come and heal his daughter. I'll never forget the change in his face when Jesus said yes. From despair to hope. I knew that change.

Extract 60
They turned to go and out of the corner of my eye I saw a woman, forcing her way through the crowd, obviously desperate. Just as Jesus turned to leave, with the last bit of strength, she finally got close enough to touch the edge of his clothes. Immediately the crowd swallowed her again, by now she was on her knees and I was afraid she would get trampled. But Jesus stopped and asked 'Who touched me?' It seemed an extraordinary question. Everyone was touching him, he could barely move for people. But he didn't mean physical touch, he meant that someone had touched him with faith, with the raw pleading that comes when all else has gone.

Part 5 - Messiah

Realising she could not hide, the woman stood up slowly, discovering as she did that she had been healed. No longer hesitant she began to pour out her story. For 12 years she had bled, drained of strength, unclean, isolated and hopeless. Until she touched Jesus.

Extract 61
Jairus was beside himself, now he knew that Jesus could heal, but instead of hurrying to his daughter, Jesus sat down with this woman and insisted that she tell him her whole story. It was wonderful to witness this woman being healed and restored. I understand isolation and loneliness - my heart melted as my son gently drew her back into society. Giving her back her body had taken a second, giving her back her dignity, her self-worth took much longer! Here with this important man waiting, Jesus gave her his full attention. I've never seen anything like it.

Extract 62
After what seemed like an age, she drew her story to a close. Fully restored she stood up, head held high, surrounded by new friends. Jesus and Jairus turned again to go to his house, but as they did so, some servants arrived from their home with dreadful news. 'There's no point troubling the teacher any more. Your daughter is dead'. It was brutal, final, in such contrast to the joy we had just witnessed. I can't imagine how Jairus must have felt. He'd seen Jesus heal, if he had gone straight away... But Jesus was calm 'Just keep believing, your daughter will be well, this death isn't the final word'. We followed of course, but only Jairus and Jesus' closest friends went into the house. I found myself standing next to Hannah, the woman who had just been healed. After a few minutes the sound of wailing from the mourners changed to shrieks then someone burst out of the house and shouted 'She's alive!' and then Jairus appeared with the little girl in his arms, clearly well and wondering what all the fuss was about. The crowd became silent and one by one we knelt in awe.

Part 5 - Messiah

Quietly Hannah turned to me and whispered 'Your son Mary, who is he?' then finally, 'Twelve years I suffered, twelve years this girl brought joy. Two people from opposite sides of society, from opposite sides of the crowd. Two of us in desperate need drawn to your son. He calms storms, casts out demons, heals the sick, raises the dead. Who is he Mary?'

Part 5 - Messiah

Behind the Diary

Luke 8: 40 - 56

As Jesus discerns the full reality of situations He is able to prayerfully discover what He should do and then empowered by the Spirit, miraculous transformation occurs. We need to do the same! Collectively discern what is going on, hear from God as to what we should do, then whether it is natural or supernatural, in faith we should get on and do it. That's basic life in the Kingdom of God: preach good news, be good news - cast out demons, heal the sick, feed the poor, raise the dead - then tell people by what power and in whose name you are doing it. It's the elementary school of the Christian faith, available for all and expected of all.

So the impressive feature of these events is not the power that God has over things - the physical world (calms the storm), the spiritual world (casts out demons), sickness (heals the woman) and death (Jairus' daughter) - nor that Jesus expects us to do these in His name. The really impressive thing is the way He gives attention to the individual even whilst addressing the big picture.

The crowds are there, hanging on His every word, yet He has a word of knowledge about the possessed man and discerns that now is the time to deal with that. He comes back and with the crowds pressing in on every side senses the difference between ordinary touch and the supernatural cry of this woman's desperation. Then Jesus discerns the bigger picture for this woman. He knows she needs more than physical healing - years of isolation means that she needs His time, His attention - and despite the urgency of Jairus' situation, He does just that. He is never rushed, never pressured, He focusses on every individual all of the time.

No matter that the universe needs His attention, His whole focus is on you right now - and forever.

Part 5 - Messiah

Mary of Magdala

Extract 63
Every year we still go to Jerusalem for Passover. The boys tell me that I shouldn't, that I'm too old for the journey. It's true that I'm almost 50 but whilst I can, I will still go. It always inspires me, I haven't lost that little girl's excitement at what God did to save his people all those years ago. And somehow I can't escape from the feeling that I am part of the story. So we go. The journey is a great time of holiday, catching up with old friends, time to talk, to try and make sense of all that is happening. And of course time to be with Jesus. Even so he spends a lot of the time with his disciples and friends but we get some wonderful moments together. We talk about happy days from the past, about his strange group of friends and recently, I tease him about Mary.

Extract 64
I like Mary, she's so wholehearted. I guess that's what has so often got her into trouble. She can't just dip her toe into anything, it has to be all or nothing. In the past, men, the occult, who knows what else. In the best times she was sneered at, mocked and abused. By the time things had got really bad she was homeless, friendless and at the mercy of everything evil. Mary of Magdala – a name used by mothers to warn daughters, by fathers to strike fear into sons. Many of my friends are surprised at how well we get on, they think I should be nervous of her influence on Jesus, wary of the rumours that might damage his growing reputation. But I like her - no, I love her. If God's plans for me had been delayed a generation, I could so easily see Gabriel standing in front of this Mary, inviting her to be the mother of God's son. But it doesn't stop me teasing Jesus! I know there can never be more than a deep friendship, a brother-sister relationship. Jesus healed her, freed her, rescued her and his calling doesn't include marriage and children.

It hurts to know this, but it doesn't stop me teasing him!

Part 5 - Messiah

Behind the Diary

Luke 8: 1 - 3

Mary of Magdala is a woman who makes a series of cameo appearances throughout the gospels. Because these glimpses are often at key moments, much has been speculated about her relationship with Jesus. Scripture tells us that 'He (Jesus) was tempted in every way common to man, yet without sin'. Here was a vulnerable young woman that Jesus frees from oppression, a woman who increasingly He restores. Inevitably this would create strong emotional ties as is borne out in the gospel accounts.

Was He tempted to cross the line from close friend to lover? Did sexually explicit thoughts ever cross His mind? Would it have been easy to arrange that private 'counselling' session? Of course. Did He long to know the intimacy of marriage? Were there times of crushing lonliness that only single people truly understand? Would He have loved children of His own? Certainly.

But did He ever cross that line, did He allow those thoughts the space they need to grow and bear fruit, did He avail Himself of the opportunities that presented themselves? No, He didn't. Did He allow the natural and right desires for marriage, intimacy, companionship, children of His own to divert Him from His calling? No He didn't. Did it hurt more than we can imagine, did it take every bit of strength, every ounce of character to remain without sin? Yes it did.

Was it easier for Jesus (being God) than it is for us? No, it was harder! Of course He could have used His divine power to resist and defeat the enemy at a stroke. But he came as Last Adam, choosing to live by faith, by the presence and empowering of the Spirit - just like us - except with the *additional* temptation to not be like us, but to take the easier road - the road which would have disqualified him from His work of redemption. Jesus loved Mary - He loves you, with a passion that holds nothing back except sin. You can too.

Part 5 - Messiah

Bethany

Extract 65
So we journey on to Jerusalem for another Passover. There was a big debate this time about whether Jesus should go - we still don't know for sure if he will celebrate in the city or whether he will stay at our friends in Bethany. The crowds love him and that offers a kind of protection, but we know the authorities are terrified that he will start a revolution. God knows the people are ready for it - if he gave the word they would fight to a man. He won't of course, I know enough to know that it isn't that kind of kingdom he keeps talking about. But even his closest friends seem convinced that he's some kind of military leader. We keep hearing what we want to hear and it can only lead to trouble.

Extract 66
We separated last night, Jesus and his disciples staying in the village, still debating whether to go to Jerusalem or not. We arrived in Bethany this morning, it is always so lovely to see Lazarus and his sisters, they have become so special to us over these last three years. So supportive of Jesus, so hospitable when the rest of the world is so demanding. Martha and Mary welcomed us with their usual warmth, but Lazarus is not well - we're hoping he'll recover enough to come with us to Passover.

Extract 67
Lazarus is worse this morning. I've seen this fever before, it's so like the one Joseph had and I'm frightened for these dear friends. I haven't said anything to the girls, but I've sent to tell Jesus.

Extract 68
Jesus still hasn't come. Mary and Martha know now that I sent for him, and still he hasn't come. Lazarus thinks that the authorities will kill him if he's anywhere near Jerusalem. This is his closest friend and Mary and Martha don't understand why he doesn't come. If I'm honest, nor do I.

Part 5 - Messiah

Behind the Diary

John 11: 1 - 6

It's alright to have friends! It's even ok to have some friends who are closer than others! In terms of ministry, Jesus has the crowds at the outpost of familiarity followed by the 72, then the wider friendship group including supporters, then the 12, then the three (Peter, James & John) and finally, John. But outside ministry, He also has some close friends with whom He can relax and share in ways and at levels that He can't with others - amongst these, Mary, Martha and Lazarus. We need to do the same. We neither need to be totally open to all or entirely closed to everyone! It's important for our health and others that we have good boundaries. But we do need some who are close enough and trusted enough to speak truth into our lives with whom we can share our highest joys and our deepest valleys. At key moments of pressure, we see Jesus retreating to this home in Bethany.

And what a moment of pressure this is for Jesus - the authorities are openly plotting against Him and Jerusalem is at the heart of the political and religious struggle. So the debate is on amongst the people, the authorities and within His disciples - should He go, would He go to Passover? Into this debate comes the unwelcome news that his best friend is worryingly ill. Now what to do? Again, the people try to decide the matter on the basis of what they can see; on the one hand there is the risk to His own safety if He goes anywhere near Jerusalem. On the other, if He doesn't His friend may die. Mary and Martha are caught up in this human, worldly way of deciding.

But Jesus has constantly pointed to a fuller way - a way that includes the bigger picture of the spiritual dimension. So He knows what to do, not on the basis of rational argument, or emotional pressure, but on the basis of Holy Spirit revelation. He has a word of knowledge about the nature of this illness, the course it will take and how the Father wants to bring good out of

Part 5 - Messiah

what the enemy has sown for harm. And on the basis of that knowledge He is able to take a decision that reason and emotion would never have allowed. With His best friend dying, He waits. What circumstances are we going through that seem inconceivable from a human perspective? Maybe, if we open our spiritual eyes, we will catch a glimpse of what God sees; victory not defeat, sight not blindness, joy instead of mourning, life instead of death.

Part 5 - Messiah

Notes:-

Part 5 - Messiah

Lazarus

Extract 69
Lazarus died during the night. It's awful. Not only do we have to cope with the grief of losing such a dear friend but there's the unspoken accusation from the girls. Your son. Our friend. Why? I have no answers. So many deaths, so much pain, so much I don't understand. Where does this end? When do we see this kingdom of yours? How much more must we endure?

Extract 70
Jesus and his disciples arrived today, four days too late. The girls wouldn't go to see him at first. Martha and Mary, the most hospitable people I know, couldn't bring themselves to welcome him. Eventually Martha went and Jesus must have said something to her because she was able to persuade Mary to greet him as well. Finally, we all went to the tomb. I watched Jesus closely. He'd been saying to everyone that Lazarus would be raised from the dead. That he'd waited until he had died so that we could all witness this greater miracle. It sounded absurd even to me. So I watched him as we drew close to the tomb. As he saw the stone, sealed and immovable, the finality of death, as he heard the women begin to weep again, tears flooded down his face. I heard the whispers. 'See how much he loved him, a pity he couldn't have come sooner and healed him'. But he hadn't wept when he heard that Lazarus had died, he seemed genuinely to believe that this could end well. So why the tears? It seemed to me that it was the scene at the tomb not the death of his friend that was moving him. Why Jesus, why?

Extract 71
I hardly need to write what happened next, everyone knows! Jesus turned to the servants and told them to roll back the stone. We were all horrified. Martha was first to react 'No, Jesus, please' then trying to think of a reason to stop this from getting any worse 'he's been dead four days, the body will have started to decompose...'. More than a reason, the hint of an accusation,

Part 5 - Messiah

a warning – you could have played a part in this, but you chose not to, now stop trying to make it alright, it's too late. But in the gentle way Jesus has, he persisted. 'Lazarus is not dead, death does not have the last word' and I remembered the little girl and hope rose in me again. I looked at Martha and held her gaze. Eventually she nodded and the servants reluctantly rolled the stone back. Jesus stepped forward, lifted his hands and prayed. Everyone was nervous, superstition mingled with anticipation but none of us was prepared for what happened. As he finished praying Jesus called out in a loud voice 'Lazarus, come out'. It was so extraordinary, yet so natural. It sounded as if he were calling to his friend to come out of the house to see something interesting.

But he wasn't, he was calling to a man four days dead. For the longest moment there was nothing. Then from the shadows, movement and Lazarus, struggling with the burial bandages stumbled into the light. No-one moved, there were no cheers, no cries, nothing. Lazarus stumbled forward and Jesus spoke gently again. 'Friends, unbind him'. Sometimes with Jesus there is a greater miracle on offer than mere healing. In our desperation to avoid the pain of death we had almost missed the joy of resurrection.

Part 5 - Messiah

Behind the Diary

John 11: 6 - 44

I wonder how many times it happens that we are deeply disappointed at God's lack of response to our heart's cry, only to later discover that He had a bigger miracle planned? It raises the question as to what the biggest miracle God can do for us is - and to answer this we need to go back to the beginning.

Triune God, lovingly in relationship within the Godhead, chooses to create you and me in order that we might share the indescribable benefits of His love. Because of the fall this relationship is no longer possible without God's intervention. But because it is so precious, not only does he stop at nothing in regard to His involvement, if we invite Him, He will stop at nothing on our behalf as well. There is no price not worth paying for the joy of eternal relationship with God. Jesus puts it like this 'better to enter the Kingdom with one eye, than have both eyes but not enter'. In picture language, Jesus is says 'together, let's do whatever it takes to have full, unhindered relationship'.

It raises a second question - what is real healing? We need God's perspective - being healed is to do with our ability to perfectly receive and perfectly give His love - anything which accomplishes this will be for our ultimate best! What if trusting Father in the midst of the physical illness will actually refine our character such that we are better able to receive His love? What should friends pray? Of course often the obvious will be right - pray for the illness to be healed!

But let's not presume that this is the case. What was best for Lazarus? What was the best for him and this beloved family in preparation for the cross that they would witness in just a few days time? Miraculous healing from a fever or the resurrection power of Christ?

Part 5 - Messiah

What are the things you wish God would deal with in your life? Is your priority the same as God's? That He would use all circumstances to bring about the very best for you - unhindered relationship with Him?

Part 5 - Messiah

Lost Things

Extract 72
What a wonderful week. Everyone wanted to talk with Lazarus, ask all the obvious questions. He just shook his head. 'One day I will die again, we must all face death, but I know that Jesus will never leave me, that he will raise me up on that last day'. And of course Jesus took the opportunity of all the visitors to carry on teaching about the kingdom. There seemed to be more urgency, not impatience exactly, but a new cutting edge to all he said. I wish I could remember it all, but I suppose that which is important to us is what we hold onto best. Looking at me He told a story of a persistent widow who nagged until she got what she wanted. No doubt he was thinking back to that wedding in Cana when I was the nagging widow! Then again the poignant story of the builder about to start building a tower. 'Would he not first pause to count the cost to see if he was able to pay the price'. He's my son; he understands so much of what I feel, what it has cost us as a family. I can barely imagine what it is costing him.

Extract 73
But my favourite was the story of the lost things. Jesus started it as any Rabbi might have, two stories with the same message, then the climax with the third story. A shepherd with a hundred sheep. That got a lot of smiles; we're only four miles from the fields of Bethlehem with thousands of sheep being prepared for Passover. But one of the sheep got lost, so the shepherd left the ninety nine and when he found the lost sheep, carried it back. He was so pleased that he had a party with his friends. That got lots of smiles too, they're a strange group, but they always enjoy a party! Then the second story following the same pattern. A woman lost one of the ten coins from her wedding headdress. She ripped the house apart until she found it, then when she did, she invited her friends round for a party. Lots more laughter. Then Jesus began the third story. We all knew how it would go, something of great worth would be lost, there would be a 'do

Part 5 - Messiah

whatever it takes' search then a party when it was found. So he began 'Once there was a man with two sons'. He didn't get any further. Peter, always impatient for the food to begin, stood up and said. 'Yes, we know, one of the sons gets lost, the Father goes off and searches for him, then when he finds him, he comes home and they have a party'.

Jesus smiled and told the story. Yes, one of the sons got lost. Yes, he was lonely and miserable and longed to be home. Yes there was a party when he returned. But nobody searched.

There was silence. If a sheep is worth seeking, if a coin is worth seeking why did he change the story when a son was lost? Why did the Father not seek?

Part 5 - Messiah

Behind the Diary

Luke 12

In this great parable Jesus sets up this fundamental question. What is God like? Is He a judge waiting to try us? An angry dictator eager to zap us, an uncaring creator willing to forget us? In a world of pain and suffering, some of our own making for sure, but pain and suffering nonetheless, what will God do? Will He do what a shepherd would do when he loses a sheep - risk all and search? Or as a woman who has lost one of the coins from her wedding dress - rip the house apart until she finds it? Jesus provokes them by suggesting that a Father might not be as compassionate, that he might stay home, passively hoping, but not actively seeking. It so fitted their understanding of a distant God, only approachable by ritual through the professionals, that it never occurred to them to question the plot.

But of course this is not what God is like! The Son of God points them to a bigger reality.

Before the foundation of the world, triune God paused on the very threshold of creation and asked 'what might this cost? Is it worth it? How far will we go if it goes wrong?'. or as Genesis puts it 'The Spirit brooded, meditated over the waters' (uncreated universe). As John literally has it in his parallel description: 'In the beginning was the conversation...' and finally as Jesus puts it: 'Which of you who was about to build a tower, would not forst stop and count the cost....'. Putting into words His own memory of that moment in eternity before when He and the Father and The Holy Spirit asked just that question. We know the answer of course - Hebrews tells us that 'For the joy that was set before him...'. God considers relationship with us worth it all!

But now it has gone wrong, sin has entered, relationship - the very point of creation, has been broken. What will God do? Judge? Ignore? Or get involved? Again, we know the answer, but

Part 5 - Messiah

when Jesus told this to the disciples they were uncertain - as are many still today. And so Jesus provokes.

Ultimately they will understand. The Father will not stand by passive, but will send His son 'to seek and to save that which was lost'. Indeed, as in the parable, the celebration, the clothes, the ring, the full cost of redemption is paid by the firstborn. Just as our salvation is won by 'the firstborn of all creation'.

Part 5 - Messiah

Palm Sunday

Extract 74
The whole crowd had gone to Jerusalem today – they were beginning to look for somewhere to celebrate Passover, there are too many of us to hold it here. They came back so excited and talking of revolution, it scared me all over again. Apparently Jesus had gone to the temple and as usual the outer courts that are supposed to be for women and non-Jews were filled with market stalls. Jesus took the belt off his coat and used it as a whip to drive off the traders, then he overturned the tables, making way for people to worship God again. So now he has the full set. All the signs the prophets told us to look for in the Messiah. Cleansing lepers, healing a man born blind, raising the dead. And now an overwhelming zeal for the house of the Lord.

The people aren't stupid, they're convinced now. So am I, I just don't think he's the sort of Messiah they're looking for. They're still hearing what they want to hear.

Extract 75
One week to Passover and the whole area is in turmoil with expectation. Jesus sent a couple of them into Jerusalem and they've come back with a donkey and the news has gone out. 'Behold your King, riding on a donkey'. We walked up from Bethany to the top of the Mount of Olives and as we came over the top the sight was amazing. Thousands of people – it seemed like the whole of Jerusalem, lining the path, hoping, waiting. Part of me wanted to join them, rejoicing that my son has found such a willing response, but most of me knows how quickly adulation can turn to hatred.

But all those thoughts were swept aside when in full view of the crowd, Jesus took this unbroken donkey, threw a blanket on it and mounted. I imagine most people expected the donkey to throw him straight off again, but instead it seemed to recognise

Part 5 - Messiah

who wanted to ride him. As they started to move down the mountain an extraordinary cheer broke from the crowd. Someone cried out 'Hosanna to the son of David, blessed is he comes in the name of the Lord' It was a cry that was taken up all round the crowd as people threw their coats into the path or cut down palm leaves to pave the way.

As we made our way down, the authorities were desperate to stop what must be looking to the Romans like the start of a revolution and demanded that Jesus silence the crowd. The donkey recognised who he was, the people recognised him. It seemed to me that even the earth recognised him. He responded 'If I tell the people to stop, the stones will cry out'.

The people cheered all the more and the authorities had no answer.

Behind the Diary

Luke 19: 28 - 48

The authorities have good reason to fear the Romans. Just a few years before Jesus' birth there had been a serious uprising amongst the Jews when many followed someone claiming to be the Messiah. It wasn't the first time, but it was the worst. Pilate almost got himself removed as Governor for his insensitive treatment of the rebels. The Roman soldiers chased the rebels until they were forced to claim sanctuary in the temple. Pilate ordered the soldiers in and they slaughtered the men by the altar. Then Pilate had the blood of the rebels mixed with the blood of the daily sacrifices and forced others to drink it, utterly defiling the temple and the religious system it represented. Israel was under its final warning - one more outbreak of rebellion and that would be the end of them as a semi-independent state within the Empire. Indeed just forty years from this point exactly that would happen.

So the authorities are right to be worried. They are desperate to shut Jesus up, but they can't afford trouble in so doing, otherwise they will precipitate the very riots they are trying to avoid. And into that dilemma comes Jesus, riding on a donkey, fulfilling the Messianic prophecy, reminding everyone of King David. Jesus of course knows where this leads, could so easily avoid it. But this is what He came for and so as the scripture has it 'he set his face towards Jerusalem and a cross'.

But all that is ahead. On this day there is a great outpouring of joy and celebration - the king is coming, the Kingdom is at hand, we are on the threshold of a new dawn.

Part 5 - Messiah

We need to recapture that sense of thrill, of anticipation. The pure delight in knowing that God is on our side and is about to break through the gloom! So often we look at the circumstances, the world trends, our personal situation and they build a picture of insurmountable problems. But Jesus can mount it! In Christ we win an overwhelming victory, so let's let our hair down, let's cut a few branches, let's exuberantly hail our King.

Nothing can stop Him! Blessed is he who comes in the name of The Lord!

Part 5 - Messiah

Passover

Extract 76
Passover at last, the sense of expectation is incredible, everyone expecting Jesus to declare himself the Messiah. Everyone thinks that in just a few days, we will be free of the Romans, free from oppression. I long to make it stop, but I know I can't. Anyway, tonight should be a welcome break from all the madness. Jesus, the family, his friends, celebrating God's goodness, the salvation of our God.

Extract 77
It was so moving. Jesus and some of his friends have gone on to Gethsemane to pray and I'm too full of such a wonderful night to sleep yet. Jesus led us through the meal. Our hosts had a young boy called John Mark and he had the honour of asking the questions 'Why this meal, why this night'. Then, as we ate, Mary came in weeping. She had a jar of perfume, I can't imagine how much it must have cost or what she must have sacrificed to buy it. But she brought it to where Jesus was. I expected her to pour a little onto his feet, I imagine everyone else thought the same. But she didn't. With a crash that silenced the room, she broke the whole jar, uncovered her head, unpinning her hair like a prostitute. Then she washed his feet with her tears and dried his feet with her hair. Finally, extravagantly, she anointed his feet with the Nard. It was such a wholehearted act of worship, so typical of this courageous woman that no one spoke for a minute. Then Judas shattered the moment complaining at the waste, but Jesus rebuked him. 'What this woman has done is beautiful and prophetic, anointing me for burial'. And then what must have cut Judas who was always looking for fame; 'Mary's name and this act of kindness will be remembered in all generations.' My heart filled with pride and love for Mary and my son, but the rage in Judas eyes disturbed me. In a moment he was gone and all that was left was the sweet fragrance of the perfume.

Part 5 - Messiah

Extract 78
Eventually, the meal continued until at the end Jesus stood and moved from his place to the spare place set as always for Elijah. Early in the meal he had shocked us by changing one of the traditional prayers when he blessed the bread, speaking of brokenness. Now he did something that had never been done before. He took the cup poured for Elijah and said 'This is the cup of the New Covenant, which is sealed in my blood, shed for many for the remission of sin' then he passed the cup to each of us to drink from. No-one knows what it means but the world seemed to stop as he spoke. A new covenant, the law fulfilled, a new beginning for us all. Perhaps there is hope in this Passover after all.

Part 5 - Messiah

Behind the Diary

Luke 22: 1 - 22

We all have choices - that's the heart of relationship. Yet the Father warns Jesus that one of the disciples will betray him. Is it inevitable, pre-planned? Is the betrayer predetermined? If so, how does choice work?

If we are going through difficult times it might be somehow reassuring to know that it is for some higher purpose and that God has it 'all under control'. But most of the time such 'control' would at best make our life meaningless and at worse, be appallingly abusive. To suggest that the awful circumstances of so many in the world are somehow for their good or for the sake of some greater plan would require God to be completely unlike the loving Father, the friend-redeemer, the comforting counselor that scripture reveals. Nor is it necessary to infer such!

The lie of the enemy, the lie that in the end the enemy is deceived by is this: A God who can do all things, must inevitably do all things. A God who wants to heal and who can heal, must therefore heal. A God who is holy and can judge, must judge. A God who wants a particular outcome and who has the absolute power to ensure it must therefore cause it to happen. It never crosses his mind that a God who is unimaginably more powerful than he would choose nonetheless to submit Himself to the degradation and death of a cross. Yet this is precisely His plan, it is exactly the path of our salvation. Omnipresent God constrains Himself to a woman's womb. Omniscient God says 'only the Father knows that'. Omnipotent God allows nails to hold Him. Jesus becomes man, our Last Adam and chooses to remain so, even when it costs Him His very life.

God could control the minute details of all our lives - predetermine every move, every word, every thought, every choice. But 'love does not insist on its own way' and God is love. This is not to say that He does not influence, not to say that He

Part 5 - Messiah

does not determine ultimate outcomes. But He does so not because He has peeked ahead and seen the outcome, nor by enforcing His will, but through the willing choices of those with whom He is in relationship.

So when Jesus says 'one of you here will betray me', he knew the disciples well, knew the way things were headed with the authorities, and knew the most likely outcomes. More, He had words of knowledge that added to this human instinct, knew hearts and motives better than the individuals themselves. But they still had free choices to make.

It could so easily have been Peter. Shortly after his great declaration that Jesus was the Christ he refuses to believe that God would die for him. 'I will die before I let that happen'. Over my dead body will I allow God to be God! No wonder Jesus replies 'get behind me Satan'. In the light of the extraordinary love and worship that Mary shows to Jesus, Judas could so easily have said 'Jesus, it's me, have mercy - now I see how much you love, how much I should love you'. We'd now be reading about Peter the betrayer and Judas the great example of humility and transformation. Yet in the light of this wonderful act of self-giving, he makes one final choice - to kill. We know it was a freely made choice and not a predestined action because Jesus attributes blame and future judgment on it. 'But woe to him who betrayed me into your hands...'

In the biggest picture of course, God does make the judgment that 'it is worth it'. But He is not the author of individual misery. Not all that happens on earth is yet His will - even though He has the power to make it so. Hence the model prayer 'your will be done on earth as it is in heaven' - recognising that currently it isn't, but inviting Him, through His people, to increasingly make it so.

Ultimately, worship is about freely choosing to trust that God is love, relying on the ultimate demonstration of that in saving us from the consequence of our and others sinful choices. Mary got it. Mary perhaps was the first to understand it. It broke her heart as surely as she broke the jar of ointment. She got it and responded freely, wholeheartedly. What about us?

Part 5 - Messiah

Notes:-

Part 5 - Messiah

Betrayal

Extract 79
They've taken him. He didn't come back last night. None of them came back. John returned late this morning, he looked terrible and I knew something awful had happened. Judas has betrayed Jesus. He brought the Sanhedrin guard to Gethsemane and accused him of treason. We don't know what has happened since, Peter tried to start a fight, but Jesus wouldn't let him, now he's disappeared along with all the others.

It can't end like this, it can't.

Extract 80
Mary's come to be with me. She says that there was some sort of hearing of the Sanhedrin last night after Jesus was arrested. I can hardly believe it, our law doesn't allow trials after sunset, how can they accuse Jesus of breaking the law when they disregard it? Surely someone will come to their senses. If only Jesus had come home.

Extract 81
There's to be another trial. The Jewish authorities are demanding the death penalty, but they're afraid of the people so they want the Romans to do it. Pilate has agreed to the hearing being outside so that we Jews don't have to become unclean by entering the court building so close the Sabbath. Why would he do that? He hates us and our traditions. He must have already agreed to kill my son. I feel sick, how can it end like this? All those promises, all those words of hope that Jesus spoke. How could they mean this?

Part 5 - Messiah

Behind the Diary

Luke 22: 39 - 62

So it comes to this. Last Adam enters a garden to face His key temptation, just as first Adam did. First Adam is tempted to be like God in attributes as well as character. Last Adam is tempted to exercise His attributes as God in order to avoid the cross.

It comes down to a choice. It was for love that this triune God created. A love founded on the unity within the trinity. Yet at the start of this final test, the will of the son is different to the will of the Father. 'Not my will, but yours...'. Now those eighteen years 'learning obedience' come into play. His will may be different to the Father's, but He is willing nonetheless to submit His will to the Father. Yet is that enough? Will redemption work on the basis of someone else making the choice - even when it is the Father? After all, it was first Adam's choice (with Eve) to act as if they had the right to God's attributes. Surely then, Last Adam must choose freely Himself not to exercise His right to them - not act on someone else's choice? The Father did not enforce His will on first Adam, how can He now impose His will on this Last Adam - even if He is willing to accept it?

And so it is. Jesus prayer is heard, but no new answer given - none is necessary. We know this because Jesus prays broadly the same thing a second time. Yet if God had answered 'It is my will' then Jesus had no need to ask again - he has already committed to do the will of the Father. If the Father says, 'no, don't do it' then again, there is no need to ask again, he already has the answer he wants. Yet He asks a second time and again receives no new answer. Finally He prays the same thing a third time and has the answer He has known all along: 'You choose' because even here, with eternity at stake, love will not insist on its own way.

Part 5 - Messiah

So Jesus goes to the disciples He has brought to the garden - tired and drunk after the long, wine filled Passover meal. He wakes them and announces that His accusers have arrived and the soldiers led by Judas enter the garden. Peter, drowsily remembering his vow 'I'll die first' pulls out his sword and tries to cut off the guard's head. But drunk and tired, succeeds only in nicking his ear. Jesus heals him and gently chides Peter, giving the answer to His prayers. 'Do you not know that even now I could ask my Father and He would send more than twelve legions of angels?'

It's Passover, they've just spent the evening remembering what one angel did - kill the firstborn of an entire nation. They know what the Father has offered - the end of the world. That's the free choice Last Adam must make. End it here or submit to a cross. 'Which of you would not first count the cost...?' Jesus counted the cost and chose in this most anguished moment, that we, you, are worth it.

This is our God, the servant King...

Part 5 - Messiah

Notes:-

The Cross

Extract 82
I'm so angry. That wasn't a trial; it was a conspiracy to murder. Our Chief Priests, Pilate and worse, the people Jesus healed, the ones he saved, the ones he has given his life to reach.. I can hardly speak about it. Pilate washed his hands. What a travesty, the man who mixed the blood of those he had killed with the Temple sacrifices, suddenly a convert to our rituals. 'What is truth' he dared ask of my son. My son is the truth! The truth is that frightened men have done what they always do. Kill and destroy what is good. But it's the ordinary people I can't understand. Jesus raised them up, he gave them real hope. But when Pilate offered to release Jesus, they asked for a thug instead. When Pilate declared himself innocent of Jesus' blood, they cursed themselves and all generations 'Let his blood be on us and on our children'. Fools! Don't they understand anything? He ordered Jesus to be beaten then crucified at noon. In less than an hour my son will be torn apart by those he loved. Mary and John tell me to stay in the house. But how can I? Of course a sword will pierce my heart, watching my son die. But the people have deserted him, his friends have deserted him. I'm his mother! How can I not be there?

Extract 83
It was strange. Awful, and yet, I don't know. More real than real. Somewhere deep inside me there is a peace, a shalom, that I can't explain. My son is dead. I watched as his tortured body collapsed under the weight of the cross. My strong carpenter, unable to carry wood. I saw the hammer raised and a thousand times in my mind saw the nails pierce his wrists. I heard the crowd taunting him, the Chief Priests mocking. I heard the silence as the cross was raised. I was there. I heard the Officer declare Jesus to be the son of God as he witnessed his dignity. I heard Jesus tell John to look after me. I stood as that supernatural darkness covered the earth.

Part 5 - Messiah

All of this should have destroyed me. But I felt as I did all those years ago when Gabriel was with me. Warmed by God's presence, peaceful even in the middle of the storm. Now, on this most holy Sabbath of the year, it is as if God is somehow with me, not allowing this bruised reed to break.

As I sit, the scriptures seem to be taking on a different shape. Jesus' words giving them new meaning. The third day he said. New wine, new wineskins, a surprising celebration on the third day.

And somewhere, beyond all reason, hope is alive in me again.

Part 5 - Messiah

Behind the Diary

Luke 22: 63 - 23: 56

Imagine, you are facing the worst hours of your life. You have no need to go through it and you have the power to avoid it. Everything within you cries out to head the other way - the people you are doing this for say the same, the old temptation 'if you are the Son of God, come down and save yourself - then we will believe'.

Nails & thorns pierce, the whip rips, the crowd you came to save taunts and spits. But worse, indescribably worse, is what transacts on the cross. The utter separation of the Son from the Father, the very definition of hell, the very opposite of the reason for creation. 'My God, my God why have you forsaken me?' The one thing that made faith feasible – the affirmation of the Father, removed leaving only the old temptation 'If you are the son of God'.

But there is more - not just the ultimate consequence of sin, but every other consequence. Every sickness, every hurt, every hatred, every death all the sin of all the world poured out on Jesus. The human frame is not designed for sin. The weight of the sin of the world corrupts, disfigures, distorts. As Isaiah puts it 'his appearance was so disfigured - beyond that of any man and his form marred beyond human likeness'. The God who came as man, who did not count equality with God a thing to be grasped, ends his life not even like man.

And He takes it all, endures it all because He believes His choice will redeem mankind. And with that He gives up the one thing that He has left. His life.

Part 5 - Messiah

Notes:-

Part 5 - Messiah

The Third Day

Extract 84
In just a few minutes it will be daybreak, the Sabbath will be over. My mind goes back to the Magi and the gifts they brought. Now of course I understand Myrrh. They knew. 'Must not the son of man suffer – and then be glorified?' How often we only hear what we want to hear.

So now, Mary and I will go to the tomb and anoint my son. Strange, I feel more for Mary than for myself. She has lost so much and had poured out so much on Jesus. How lost she looks. For her sake, I need to do this with her.

Extract 85
As we approached the tomb in the half-light, for a moment it seemed as if we were back at Bethany, outside Lazarus' tomb. Now I understood why Jesus had wept. Not for his friend who would soon be raised, but for death itself. For those who would, just a few days later, be stood outside his tomb.

My thoughts were scattered a moment later as an earthquake hit the garden. Both of us fell and when the dust settled we saw that the guards had gone and the stone was rolled away. A thrill went through my heart 'even the stones recognise him', but Mary was distressed assuming something even worse had happened. When we reached the tomb we couldn't see inside, it was still too dark, but one thing was clear. Jesus was not there. As we turned around two angels stood in place of the guards and asked simply 'Why do you seek the living amongst the dead?' Again my heart raced, could it really be? But Mary could not be consoled, could not hear anything other than what her mind and heart had told her for years. 'You are a worthless woman, nothing good ever happens for you – and when it does it is taken away'. Gently I led her back to the house, quietly giving thanks to God, frightened that my heart would overflow and sweep me away.

Part 5 - Messiah

Extract 86

I'm in the house alone for a few minutes. Peter had come back whilst Mary and I were out. He looked ashamed and as soon as I told them about the empty tomb, he and John ran off for something to do. Mary couldn't stand the silence so she too has gone back to the garden.

But I don't need to. I know. It's the third day. I know Jesus, he'll deal with the boys later. But he'll want some time with Mary first. She needs healing, restoring. She needs to know that he will always be there for her.

That's what Jesus does. He puts the universe to one side to focus on the one. And he does it for everyone. A new covenant, in his blood. A new beginning, a new freedom, a new wholeness from his broken body.

It's getting light. The light of the world is back and nothing can ever put it out..

Behind the Diary

John 20:1-18

Have you understood along with Mary? That Jesus' gaze is upon you right now? Have you understood along with David? That the omnipotent Lord of all creation bends all His power, all his knowledge, all His reach to this one end - to shepherd you personally into His presence?

Why are you still reading this? The light of the word is here waiting to speak your name and welcome you into His joy. Go spend time with Him!

Part 6 - Kingdom

Notes:-

Part 6 - Kingdom

Beach Barbeque

Extract 87
These are strange but wonderful days. Jesus keeps appearing to us and the other disciples, teaching more about what has just happened and preparing us for what is to come. Mary is utterly transformed! From a broken woman without any sense of self-worth she has a grace and assurance that makes me understand 'shalom' in a new and deeper way.

Jesus gave her back her dignity - more, he gave all women a new calling. 'Tell my brothers' he told her in the garden. Jesus, God's son, entrusting this 'sinful' woman with the greatest news, the highest truth there will ever be. Mary, teach the men! At first Peter was offended, but it quickly passed - he is too aware of his own inability to handle truth right now to worry about it.

Extract 88
Of course, I'm staying with John now. I'm sure he'd rather be with Peter and James, planning where they will go and how they will change the world! They still don't quite understand Jesus' ways yet, but they are getting there slowly! We've just come back from the beach - I went to welcome John and the boat after the night's fishing - and to see if there were any fish for breakfast! When I got there I could see that there was already a fire and someone was cooking fish. Jesus waved me to join him. I needn't have worried about the food, there was so much! He seems so much more relaxed, we have time to talk, mother and son and so much more than that.

The nail prints in his hand a permanent reminder of just how much more.

Extract 89
Finally the boat appeared in the half-light and we heard the men wondering who was on the beach. When John realized it was

Part 6 - Kingdom

Jesus he quickly got his dry clothes from the stern of the boat and began to get dressed. Peter of course couldn't wait he just dived into the water all but naked!

He seemed to have second thoughts as he climbed onto the beach to face Jesus - it must have been the first time they had had time to speak personally since Jesus' resurrection. How close Peter had come to being the one to betray Jesus. When he told the servant girl that he didn't know Jesus he was telling more of the truth than he knew. Of course if he'd really known my Jesus, he wouldn't have been worried about meeting him half naked!

Sound carries so far along the beach, reflected from the water. We didn't mean to hear, but Jesus put his arm around Peter and asked simply 'do you now love me for who I am Peter, or are you still insisting on me being who you think I should be?' Peter almost choked as he answered. 'Jesus, you know I am your friend'. Jesus nodded and said 'Then feed my sheep.' Peter was in turmoil, not knowing what it meant or what to do. Jesus called after him: 'Peter, do you love me without conditions?' Peter, so aware of his great professions of faith in the past and his failure to deliver when it mattered couldn't bring himself to make such a promise. 'Jesus, you know me. I'm your friend'. From the anguish it was causing him I'm sure he felt that it was an admission of failure. Jesus didn't see it like that: 'Feed my lambs' he said.

Then before Peter could respond he lowered his voice so that we could barely hear: 'Peter, are you really my friend?' That did it. All inhibitions gone, all fear of rejection cast aside, he crumpled in front of Jesus: 'Jesus, you know all things you know that I am your friend'. Jesus pulled Peter to his feet and hugged him: 'Then feed my sheep. Peter, you once told me that you would die to stop me suffering. Now, one day you will die to share in my suffering.'

Behind The Diary

John 21:1-19

What was it that stopped Jesus from being the one to betray Jesus? He came so close. Like Judas he had his own fixed ideas about what the Messiah should do, what he would be like. He was creating God in his own image and insisting that He behave appropriately. It's dangerous ground - 'get behind me Satan' Jesus said. Yet in the end, something pulls him back whereas with Judas it pushes him forward. One repents, one regrets. One builds the kingdom, the other excludes himself from it.

Ultimately it has to do with wholehearted transparency. Peter might think the wrong thoughts, might behave outrageously, might have no real idea. But it's always visible, always in the light, always open to the prayerful intervention of friends and God Himself. This story highlights these factors. He jumps out of the boat half-naked - nothing covered! He's open, wholehearted in his desire to be with the man who means so much to him. When challenged about the level and integrity of his love, he is open and honest, unwilling to say more than he can guarantee. He has learned from the past who he is and where his flaws lie and he doesn't care who knows. That's the definition of confession and repentance. It makes him trustworthy and useable and so Jesus restores him.

Not so with Judas. It's all hidden, all inside, all in the dark - inaccessible to anyone else, fundamentally unaccountable. It's a sad, sad story for Judas - yet so typical of those who remain closed to outside influence. Peter's story on the other hand encourages us: It' s not about where we are on the journey that precludes us from significant ministry, it's how we are allowing ourselves to be shaped.

Who are you accountable to? Do you feel like you are disqualified from ministry because of the past? Listen again to Peter's story and be encouraged!

Part 6 - Kingdom

Notes:-

Part 6 - Kingdom

Ascension

Extract 90

Jesus has told us all to meet him on the Mount of Olives. He hasn't met with all of us since Passover. We've all wondered why he hasn't just appeared to the authorities to prove them wrong once and for all. But he's never been in the business of proving anything! He longs for us to be friends with him and with his Father and you can't do that on the basis of proof and evidence. So for those who wouldn't believe, who wouldn't trust, he won't force them by standing in front of them!

We have some friends who live in Emmaus and they were going home after the Passover weekend – distraught at what had happened to Jesus. As they were walking a 'stranger' joined them and explained how 'the Christ must suffer'. They were amazed at his insight and felt closer to God than they had ever done before – they didn't realize they were walking next to Him! When they got to Emmaus, Jesus made as if to continue – he'd revealed enough of himself to begin a relationship, now they had to choose to take the next step – he wouldn't impose himself. I'm so glad they invited him in, so often in my life a lack of hospitality has led to pain and separation. But not this time, as Jesus shared a meal with them and broke bread, they recognized him for who he was. That's the way it works, a gradual revelation, a step of faith then a full revealing. Hopeless, they had walked away from Jerusalem, the Place of Peace. But now, friends with Jesus, they are back here, full of hope, waiting on the hillside with the rest of us for one final meeting.

Part 6 - Kingdom

Extract 91
He's gone – as we watched he was lifted into heaven. Still my son, yet so much more. The Son of God, just as Gabriel told me. He said that only if he left could the Holy Spirit come, he said that it was better for us that way. He said he would be with us always, even to the end of this age. But my son is gone and for now I can't see beyond that.

Extract 92
John seems to understand how I feel – how he has changed! Still the 'son of thunder', still with that zeal, that strength and focus, but more than any of the others, he seems to know my Jesus. Peter seems to be taking the lead, but it's John who is holding the ship on course! Jesus told us that he had been given all authority and that we were to go into the whole world and make disciples of all nations. Many of the men thought that was a mandate to go and start a revolution. Peter knew that wasn't what he meant but it was John who explained it. In any case, Jesus told us to wait in Jerusalem until we receive authority from the Holy Spirit before we do anything. No one knows exactly what that means or how long we must wait.

I know about waiting, but the others aren't quite there yet!

Part 6 - Kingdom

Behind The Diary

Acts 1: 1-14

So here is Jesus, resurrected, fully entitled now to exercise His rights as God. With one word, all the nations would fall at His feet, in an instant He could enforce His will on a sinful world. In a moment He could be vindicated and revenged against those who so cruelly rejected Him. At the very least, He could appear to all those who disbelieved, proving His deity once and for all. Yet even now He refuses to do so. Instead, He entrusts us with the project of communicating, demonstrating and establishing the Kingdom. That which He had the right to do, He chooses instead to do through us. It brings us a significance that we neither deserve nor have the capacity in ourselves to achieve. Yet for our sake, He makes it so.

In Eden, God first gives mankind authority; 'have dominion..' But we gave it away to the enemy of our souls so that he became 'the Prince of This World'. Now, at extraordinary cost, Jesus has won back the authority; 'all authority in heaven and earth has been given to me...'

Consider how much trust and significance He places in you as He looks you in the eye and says; 'Go therefore...' He gives the church the authority, empowered by the Spirit. He calls you.

Part 6 - Kingdom

Notes:-

Part 6 - Kingdom

Pentecost

Extract 93
It's as if he's back! We were gathered together as we've done so many times these last weeks – waiting, praying, worshiping God. It was the same room we had shared that final Passover in. I was just thinking how strongly I could feel Jesus' presence and as I closed my eyes I could see Him wildly running around, chasing the children or play-fighting with his friends. Then suddenly I realised that it was real. I opened my eyes to see what looked like a storm in the room. A wild, untamed wind blew around us and flames, fanned by the wind seemed to dance on each person. It wasn't frightening, it was playful and powerful, uncontrolled yet ordered. I recognised that kind strength. My mind turned back to what John had said: 'he will baptise you with the Spirit and with fire'.

My heart leaped. It was Jesus, it was God. I went to shout out my news to the others in the room, but as I opened my mouth a joy welled up from deep within me and I began to worship God in a language I had never heard before. We were so excited that we spilled out of the house into the street – going up to strangers and telling them the extraordinary news that Jesus is alive and that he has come back forever!

Extract 94
At first the people didn't understand what was happening, most assumed we were drunk – babbling in languages they didn't understand. But as things settled down it became obvious what God was doing. Jerusalem was full of people from all nations and whatever their native language, one of was proclaiming Jesus in their language. Peter took the lead and using his booming voice explained it: 'These people aren't drunk – it's only mid-afternoon'. To be honest, knowing some of Jesus friends, that wouldn't have persuaded me, but he went on: 'this is what Joel said "in these last days, God will pour out his Spirit on all

Part 6 - Kingdom

people... and they will prophecy" God is proclaiming his goodness, his plan to everyone in their own language – now you have no excuse'. It was incredible – Peter speaking with knowledge, teaching from scripture with authority. Just days ago he was a broken man, unsure of himself, convinced he was useless to God. Now here he was, filled and anointed by the Spirit of Jesus, feeding his sheep.

Extract 95
I wake up every day with Jesus! No more goodbyes, no more anxiety about what will happen next to him. No more times of loneliness when he was away with his disciples. 'I will be with you always' he said – and he meant it! But it's so much more than having him in the house with me. Of course that's wonderful and fills me with joy every new day, but it's as if I can see in colour now rather than in shades of grey. Now when I look ahead I can see not only with my eyes, but with a spiritual sight that I can't explain. God giving me knowledge and wisdom beyond anything I could have seen with my eyes or understood with my mind. And the certainty of his presence gives me the confidence to act on that insight. Knowing he will pick me up if I fall, redirect me if I go the wrong way.

And it isn't just me – it's everyone who lets my son touch them with his love! And that's more and more people every day – small groups of friends, families, whole villages, even some of the priests and leaders of the people. It seems like everyone is finally rejoicing that Jesus is alive – and being transformed to be like him as his Spirit grabs hold of them!

Behind The Diary

Acts 2: 1-47

Jesus said that it would be better for us if He left in person and returned through the Spirit. He meant it. He said to His disciples 'greater things than these will you do'. He meant it.

The incarnate Son of God took on humanity and lived within those limitations. Just like us He lives His life in the flesh empowered by the Spirit. All that He did, all that He was, in potential, we can be. Moreover, there was only one Jesus on earth, limited in capacity by His humanness. Now through His Spirit, He can empower all believers, multiplying His effectiveness throughout the world.

Now, no longer bounded by the limitations of one body, Jesus can be real and present through His body to the whole world, all the time. Through you, with you, in you.

So many times I have heard 'It was easier for the disciples, they had Jesus with them'. That isn't Jesus' view and it isn't the living experience of countless believers! Are you in touch with the dynamic, living presence of Jesus day by day? Are you living your life in the technicolour fullness that the Spirit brings? Are you making decisions on the basis of spirit-given insight? Are you experiencing eternal life, life in all its fullness?

The promise is for you, not for someone else, someone more holy, someone more special. For you. For all who will follow Jesus. If you are not experiencing it, find someone to pray with today.

Part 6 - Kingdom

Notes:-

Part 6 - Kingdom

Transformers

Extract 96

I can't stop laughing! John and I have just come home after walking around the city. Peter and the others wanted a revolution and they've got one - but so much more profound than they ever imagined possible. They wanted the drama of violently replacing one authority for another - in the end nothing much would have changed. Instead through these ecclesia, little groups of people brought to real life by the Spirit of Jesus, the city is unrecognisable. Sworn enemies holding out hands in genuine friendship, families reconciled after years of hurt, sicknesses and evil spirits being cast out - the oppressed being set free. Real life is flooding back, John tells me that the whole economy of Jerusalem is being transformed - people aren't buying as much because they are sharing what they have meaning they have more money to give to the poor. I've noticed it already - there aren't as many beggars or homeless people. Of course it means that some corrupt businesses aren't doing as well and although people are going to the Temple in even bigger numbers, they aren't buying sacrifice animals as much - they don't need to, Jesus is their sacrifice. Just weeks ago, Jesus had to use force to get rid of the traders so that the women and Gentiles could worship. Today the traders had gone and the courts were full of all nations praising God.

Jesus did amazing miracles over these last three years, but this is even more extraordinary. This fire isn't just changing a few lives. This could change the world and I don't think even the powers of hell can stop it.

Part 6 - Kingdom

Extract 97

Of course, there are some who still refuse to see what is in front of their eyes. All they see is a loss of income or an eroding of authority – they don't see that it was income from ungodly business or authority based on power & tyranny - but nonetheless, eventually they will fight back I'm sure. Even now, in the midst of this incredible blessing there are complaints! Those who a few weeks ago had nothing, now complaining that they aren't receiving as much as others! Of course, until they receive the real gift, their stomachs may be better fed, but their hearts will remain cold, immune to the warming love of Jesus.

Peter and the others have appointed seven administrators to help distribute the food and money being given to help the poor. I understand the reason, but we're supposed to be a radically new kingdom rooted in the love of God – and it's working! If we're not careful we'll simply become an alternative to the old priesthood and synagogue system.

Part 6 - Kingdom

Behind The Diary

Acts 5:12 - 6:7

It seemed a crazy plan. Instead of God doing it Himself, using His power to overturn the world system, He chooses to use these nobodies, this dysfunctional group of largely uneducated men and women. And so few of them! How can such a small number achieve such an ambitious goal? Little wonder that the disciples thought of Jesus, the Messiah, as a military leader. How else do you overturn such a powerful force as the Romans? But of course God's plan is much bigger than even this. He wants to overturn the Prince of this World, he wants to transform men's hearts. If the physical task seemed impossible with this small rabble, how much more impossible is God's agenda?

Yet generation after generation, we see societies transformed. We see evil overturned, we see the enemy cast out, lives set free and hearts changed. Through people like us. Through churches like ours. It should be the most exciting, thrilling adventure, captivating our whole being and shaping our life. It brings joy, meaning, significance, hope, freedom. It makes all the difference in the world - are you a part of it yet?

Of course the risk always is to try and capture it and put it in a bottle. We codify it, legislate for it, institutionalise it - find ways to imprison it, box it and make it human shaped. The Apostles saw that they were getting overwhelmed with the detail and set up the first admin team. Nothing wrong with that, but as we shall see, the next time we see these deacons is not in their admin role but as they preach and evangelise. Good administration is a God given gift that facilitates ministry. Just don't be surprised when your best administrators metamorphose into evangelists, teachers and church planters!

Part 6 - Kingdom

Don't box God, either in your concept of who He is or what He should do. Don't box church by thinking of it as an institution or a set of structures or a doctrinal statement.

God is living, dynamic, untamable. Get in the jet-stream of His love and purposes. Be being filled with the Spirit and enjoy the ride!

Part 6 - Kingdom

Stephen

Extract 98
Maybe I was unduly worried – God is big enough to break out of the tombs we lock him in! Stephen, one of the seven administrators has been preaching about Jesus everywhere he goes – so much so that the authorities have ordered him to stop. I love it! The enemy tries to stop the kingdom being born by killing my son. But God raises him to life creating more courageous support for the kingdom than there was before! Then when the kingdom is growing faster than any of us believed possible the enemy tries to slow it down with bureaucracy, but God uses those appointed to administer it to become catalysts for even faster growth. The enemy can't win!

Extract 99
But he can still hurt us. Stephen was killed yesterday. It reminded me so much of Jesus – you could see where it was leading, but no amount of persuasion could deflect him from doing what was right. He was preaching in the market place as they distributed food to the poor, telling people the extraordinary story of Jesus, his life, his death, his resurrection. Then a group from the synagogue of free men (who were actually slaves of the enemy) and one of the rising stars of the Pharisees began to argue with him. Saul, the Pharisee, has been opposing and persecuting believers all over the region and is obviously looking to make a name for himself here in the Capital. After a while it must have become clear that they could not defeat Stephen's arguments, so they went and accused him before the High Priest. John & I went to the trial to support Stephen. I could see where it would end. Nothing could stop Stephen. He spoke the most powerful sermon I have ever heard. Starting with Abraham, he explained how God has always given Himself for His people and how we have always ended up rejecting His offer of love. He finished by explaining how Jesus was the incarnation of God's love and that this generation had acted just like all the

Part 6 - Kingdom

others – rejecting, not just his messengers, but this time, His very son. It was too much for the authorities. Enraged at Stephen's accusation of them, they confirmed his accusation – by killing another of God's messengers. A man so filled with God's love, with the Spirit of Jesus that his face, even when he was being stoned, looked like an angel. I will never forget his final words: "Behold, I see the heavens opened up and Jesus standing at the right hand of God. Lord, do not hold this sin against them!"

Part 6 - Kingdom

Behind the Diary

Acts 6:8 - 7:60

This is the transforming power of God. Stephen, a man who had never met Jesus prior to His resurrection, knows Jesus intimately well. The Spirit has led him into all truth through the Old Testament scriptures and now through His own indwelling of this Godly man. So much so that when it comes to the final choice - to continue preaching and die or stop and live, he gladly chooses death. That's the choice Jesus has won for each of us. How will we die? Will it be in the countless little deaths resulting from sin and ending with eternal death or in a choosing to lay down our agenda, our life in order to have the life of Jesus raise us to eternal, abundant life?

This is where it starts and where it ends. In Eden, the choice between life and death. In Gethsemane, the choice between life and death. Not all of us will face the choice physically, but we all face it. Faith that saves is faith that takes the ultimate risk, that throws itself on God. That says 'even if I die, I will trust that God is as He says He is. All other choices than that final one can be overturned. But death draws the curtain on choices. Everything rests on the choice we make facing death. But how do we prepare for that? Rarely is it that great leap from nothing to this. It's in the day by day dying to self; choosing someone elses agenda rather than our own, choosing to respond graciously rather than angrily, choosing to worship when we feel down, choosing to be generous when we don't have enough, choosing to love when we have been hated. It's in choosing to look away rather than entertain lust, it's in not watching what everyone else watches, not claiming that expense that all your friends have claimed. It's in standing up for what is right, for the poor and oppressed when the stones get thrown at you as well. It's in dying to your own reputation for the sake of those who are vulnerable. In a countless stream of dying to self that becomes a rushing torrent of choices, the waterfall of physical death becomes simply the next choice rather than the last choice.

Part 6 - Kingdom

Jesus said it 'take up your cross daily'. Paul alluded to it 'not that I have yet reached this goal, but I press on'. The writer to the Hebrews knew it 'therefore, let us also run with perseverance the race that is set before us, looking to Jesus, the pioneer and perfector of our faith'. Stephen knew it and saw Jesus welcoming him into full, abundant, eternal life.

What choices do you face today that will shape that final choice?

Part 6 - Kingdom

The Diary

Extract 100

It's strange, the more the authorities persecute Jesus, the more people follow 'the way'. The more the world hates, the more God's love takes root - every day more people become believers, sharers in Jesus' love. And so many of them want to meet me. Somehow they seem to think that seeing me will make my son more real. Of course it doesn't, his Spirit makes him more real than any amount of my stories. But I love meeting them, their wonder, their joy as they experience real freedom, encounter God's love afresh in their lives.

So many people, I scarcely get any time to write now - in any case my eyes aren't what they used to be and it all takes longer. But I'm glad I've written this diary, it helps me get it right when I tell the new believers what it was really like, to lead them to the truth about my Jesus.

And today I am especially glad. I met someone different. Someone who I think will be significant in this new kingdom. Peter himself brought him to John and me. His name is Luke, he's a doctor and a devout believer. But like so many, he's now heard so many stories about Jesus that he doesn't know which are true, or if they are true, what they mean. He wants to write an orderly account so that everyone can know the truth and not be distracted or diverted from a genuine relationship with Jesus.

He wants to read my diary.

Part 6 - Kingdom

Dear lover of God,

Many people have put together accounts of what God has done among us recently, listening to the stories told by those who saw these things with their own eyes. In the excitement it can be quite confusing, so I decided to start again, doing my own careful research, in order to compile an accurate, ordered account so that you may know the truth about the things you have been taught.

It started in the days of Herod, king of Judea when a priest named Zechariah (part of the Abijah division) was married to a descendant of Aaron (another priest!) called Elizabeth. They were both making right choices before God, walking blamelessly in all the requirements of the Lord. Yet they had no children and were both passed the point where this seemed possible. Now it happened that whilst his division was on duty, Zechariah was chosen by drawing lots to enter the temple for the daily ritual of burning incense (symbolic of the people's prayers ascending to God). Whilst he was doing this, an angel of the Lord appeared to him, standing at the right of the altar of incense! Zechariah was frightened but the angel told him not to be afraid but that his prayers had been heard and that he and Elizabeth would have a son to be called John. He went on to say that this would bring great joy not only to him and Elizabeth but to many because his birth would be a sign to the people that God's Messiah was soon to come. For this reason he was to be distinctive - God would play his part in that he would be filled with the Holy Spirit from his conception, they were to play theirs by giving him nothing alcoholic to drink.

Zechariah would not take the angel at his word and asked for proof, pointing out that he was an old man and that Elizabeth was well passed child-bearing age. Exasperated, the angel responded: 'I am Gabriel, I stand in the very presence of God and was told to bring this good news to you. But now, because of

Part 6 - Kingdom

your unbelief, you will be unable to tell this good news until the words are fulfilled.' The people were waiting for Zechariah to come out, puzzled at the delay, but of course he couldn't tell them and eventually went home to Elizabeth. After this Elizabeth became pregnant but kept herself secluded, filled with joy that God had taken away the shame people had for those who were childless.

In the sixth month of her pregnancy, Gabriel was sent from God to a city in Galilee called Nazareth, to a virgin contracted in marriage to a man whose name was Joseph, of the descendants of David;

and the virgin's name was Mary.....

Part 6 - Kingdom

Behind the Diary

Luke 1

I hope this journey through the gospel story from Mary's perspective has inspired you in your own journey. The wonderful thing is that it isn't just a story, it happened. It's not like a film where you get to the end, dry your eyes and leave the warmth of the imaginary world for the harsh reality of the real one. The gospel message is that you get to take the warmth, the joy, the peace, the excitement with you. The gospel message is that the life and power of Jesus can live in and through you, transforming the harsh reality into the bigger reality of God's redemptive love and purposes.

When Luke finishes his account at the end of Acts it's as if there are chapters yet unwritten - it just stops. That's because there are unwritten chapters. And some of those tell the story of what God accomplished in and through you. What's your story, what will it tell, what are the angels already whispering about it? What can it become, what is there still to write?

Wherever you are, whatever you have done, the gospel is simple. Starting right now you can rewrite history. You can start afresh this minute on a journey of significance and wonder. Just as with Mary when Gabriel first spoke, God is now speaking to you by His Holy Spirit. I don't know the precise words; they are unique to each individual. But I know the gist. 'Don't be afraid, God is with you, follow Him, let Him direct your paths, let Him fill you with life'. Can I encourage you to respond along with Mary?

'Let it be to me as you have said'

Other 'Mary's Diary' Opportunities

If you have enjoyed this written version of Mary's Diary you may be interested in the other formats of the 'Diary'.

Firstly an Audio version comprising dramatic readings of the Diary together with songs from the musical production is available on CD.

Secondly there are a variety of stage productions suitable for churches, schools and theatres. These include;

Solo pieces that are ideal for school assemblies, RS and other lessons or in church youth group settings. These all use pre-recorded backing tracks and can be tailored to suit timing and theme by selecting the extracts to be performed.

A two-person version covering the complete diary, either as two one hour performances or as one production with an interval. This can be used as a theatre style event or within two church services. In either case a pre-recorded backing track is usually used for the music.

A full musical production including script, staging notes, choreography and music is also available as an Easter evangelistic event.

For more details of any of these please visit our website www.marysdiary.net

Acknowledgements

Mary's Diary is written by David Painting © 2008

'Behind the Diary' notes written by David Painting © 2009

Songs in the musical versions by Adrian Snell from the Albums; 'The Virgin' © 1981, 'The Passion' © 1980 (used by permission)

Solo performances and staging by Sarah Foulkes